A Complete Guide to the
Level 4 Certificate in Education & Training

SECOND EDITION

FURTHER EDUCATION

D1427616

You might also like the following books in our *Further Education* series

The A-Z Guide to Working in Further Education
Jonathan Gravells and Susan Wallace
978-1-909330-85-6 Published 2013

A Complete Guide to the Level 5 Diploma in Education and Training
Lynn Machin, Duncan Hindmarch, Sandra Murray and Tina Richardson
978-1-909682-53-5 Published 2014

Equality and Diversity in Further Education
Sheine Peart
978-1-909330-97-9 Published 2014

Inclusion in Further Education
Lydia Spenceley
978-1-909682-05-4 Published 2014

The Professional Teacher in Further Education
Keith Appleyard and Nancy Appleyard
978-1-909682-01-6 Published 2014

Reflective Teaching and Learning in Further Education
Nancy Appleyard and Keith Appleyard
9781909682856 Published 2015

Teaching and Supporting Adult Learners
Jackie Scruton and Belinda Ferguson
978-1-909682-13-9 Published 2014

Understanding the Further Education Sector: A Critical Guide to Policies and Practices
Susan Wallace
978-1-909330-21-4 Published 2013

Our titles are available in a range of electronic formats. To order please go to our website www.criticalpublishing.com or contact our distributor, NBN International, 10 Thornbury Road, Plymouth PL6 7PP, telephone 01752 202301 or email orders@nbninternational.com.

A Complete Guide to the
Level 4 Certificate in Education & Training

SECOND EDITION

**LYNN MACHIN, DUNCAN HINDMARCH,
SANDRA MURRAY & TINA RICHARDSON**

FURTHER
EDUCATION

First published in 2013 by Critical Publishing Ltd
Reprinted in 2014
Second edition published in 2015

The authors have made every effort to ensure the accuracy of information
contained in this publication, but assume no responsibility for any errors,
inaccuracies, inconsistencies and omissions. Likewise every effort has been
made to contact copyright holders. If any copyright material has been reproduced
unwittingly and without permission the Publisher will gladly receive information
enabling them to rectify any error or omission in subsequent editions.

British Library Cataloguing in Publication Data
A CIP record for this book is available from the British Library

ISBN: 978-1-910391-09-9

This book is also available in the following e-book formats:

MOBI ISBN: 978-1-910391-10-5
EPUB ISBN: 978-1-910391-11-2
Adobe e-book ISBN: 978-1-910391-12-9

The rights of Lynn Machin, Duncan Hindmarch, Sandra Murray and Tina
Richardson to be identified as the Authors of this work have been asserted
by them in accordance with the Copyright, Design and Patents Act 1988.

Text design by Greensplash Limited
Cover design by Out of House Ltd
Project Management by Out of House Publishing
Printed and bound in Great Britain by Bell & Bain, Glasgow

Critical Publishing
152 Chester Road
Northwich
CW8 4AL
www.criticalpublishing.com

MIX
Paper from
responsible sources
FSC FSC® C007785
www.fsc.org

Contents

Praise for the first edition

User friendly, easy to read and covered a good range of material with good examples and case studies.

Kerry Adam
South Staffordshire College

The study skills section is very good - it picks up on the main issues facing trainees in Education and Training contexts and ensures that the advice and guidance are directly relevant to these learners. Also good are the sections on teaching observations and progression.

Paul G Daniels
Dearne College

It is a useful and accessible text which provides student teachers with reflective activities to enhance the learning they do ... It's advantage is accessibility for Level 4 requirements of study.

Trish Spedding
University of Sunderland

I ... would certainly put this on the reading list and offer it as a key text as it is easy to understand and suitable for learners of that level.

Lula Rendall
Truro Penwith College

I particularly liked the activities to check understanding and the references to the criteria.

Joanne Byrne
South Leicestershire College

I like the accessibility and particularly the chapter on communication.

Vanessa Cottle
University of Derby

I will be recommending it for its simplicity as a core text for our new ITT introductory programme.

Christian Beighton
Canterbury Christchurch

Acknowledgements

We would like to thank our families, friends and colleagues for the support that they have given us during the writing of this book.

We would also like to thank our publishers, Julia Morris and Di Page, for their friendliness, professionalism and on-going support.

Thanks also to you for reading this book. We hope that you enjoy reading it and best wishes with your studies.

Lynn, Duncan, Sandra and Tina, 2015

Meet the authors

Lynn Machin is an award leader, senior lecturer and a PhD, EdD, MA supervisor within the School of Education at Staffordshire University. She has more than 25 years' experience of working within further and higher education with many of these years spent designing and delivering initial teacher training for trainees who work, or want to work, in the further education sector. Her post-doctoral research interests are situated in the exploration of how students can develop their capacities to learn and grow as self-directed and autonomous learners. As well as having written and co-authored several books for teachers within FE; including *A Complete Guide to the Level 5 Diploma in Education and Training*, Lynn has also written several other books including *Supporting Primary Teaching and Learning* (for teaching assistants).

Duncan Hindmarch is award leader for and senior lecturer within the School of Education at Staffordshire University. With a background in teaching English for speakers of other languages (ESOL), he has over 17 years of teaching experience. Duncan is a Senior Fellow of the Higher Education Academy and has led development and implementation of ESOL, initial teacher training (ITT) and education programmes. As well as having written and co-authored several books for teachers within FE, including *A Complete Guide to the Level 5 Diploma in Education and Training*, Duncan has also contributed to *Supporting Primary Teaching and Learning*, aimed at primary teaching assistants.

Sandra Murray is a lecturer within the School of Education at Staffordshire University. Sandra, having taught for many years in a further education college, has a wide range of experience supporting and teaching teachers in the further education sector and has been teaching on initial teacher education programmes since 2006. Her particular research interest is inspirational and outstanding teaching. She has written and co-authored several books for teachers within FE; including *A Complete Guide to the Level 5 Diploma in Education and Training*.

Tina Richardson is also an award leader and senior lecturer within the School of Education at Staffordshire University. Tina has taught in compulsory education, further education and higher education. For the past 15 years she has been involved in teacher training for FE, in particular the subject specialist qualifications for teachers. Her particular research interest is the use of metacognitive reading strategies in the functional skills classroom. As well as teacher training books, including *A Complete Guide to the Level 5 Diploma in Education and Training*; Tina has also co-authored a book on using e-readers in the classroom.

You can find more information about the authors, their research areas as well as useful information about the further and higher education sectors on their website: **www.teachwriteresearch.com**

Preface

Welcome to this book. It has been written with you, the teacher, in mind. We wish you all the best with your studies and every success as a teacher.

About this book

Training to be a teacher within the further education and skills sector can be an exciting and transforming learning experience. Studying for a level 4 Certificate in Education and Training (CET) qualification is part of that process of transformation. The intention of this book is to support you in your studies as you make this transition and as you work towards achieving your CET qualification. It does this through:

- ○ coverage of all of the core units that are in the level 4 CET qualification;

- ○ alignment of chapters to the standards underpinning the level 4 CET qualification;

- ○ encouraging you to reflect upon your practice;

- ○ providing case study scenarios and examples;

- ○ indicating sources of information for further in-depth study;

- ○ being research informed and written by teacher educators with teachers' needs in mind.

The topics, questions and activities within this book have been tailored to the demands of the qualification and are aligned to the Education Training Foundation (ETF) standards framework around which the level 4 CET qualification has been designed. In addition to this you will find a chapter that focuses on helping you to become a reflective practitioner. You will also find a chapter that provides coverage of key study skills, including advice about reading critically, note taking, presenting your work and referencing correctly.

Each chapter begins by providing a visual concept map of the topics to be covered as well as a list of the chapter's objectives. Points for pre-flection are followed by detailed text accompanied by questions and activities that will provide you with an opportunity to check your understanding and assess your learning. Case studies bring the text to life and show how the theory can be applied in practice. At the end of each chapter you will find a summary of the main ideas and suggestions for further reading.

Suggested answers for some of the activities can be found at the back of the book, along with a helpful glossary of acronyms and useful templates for key documents.

Lynn, Duncan,
Sandra and Tina, 2015

Introduction: Historical background to the further education and skills sector and the level 4 Certificate in Education and Training qualification

KEY WORDS

certificate, CET, credits, CTLLS, DTLLS, education, ETF, FE, FENTO, government, level, LLUK, LSIS, policy, qualification, training.

INTRODUCTION

If you have picked up this book then it is likely that you are about to embark on the level 4 Certificate in Education and Training (CET) qualification which is aimed at developing your skills as a teacher within the further education (FE) and skills sector. Of course, there are some very specific things you will need to learn about teaching, but it is also important that you have some background information about the sector you are about to enter. This introductory chapter aims to meet the following objectives:

○   to provide you with an understanding and appreciation of the historical background that led to the introduction of the level 4 CET qualification;

○   to explain the purpose of the level 4 CET qualification;

○   to outline the requirements of the level 4 CET qualification.

Terminology

Post-compulsory education refers to all education undertaken by learners aged 16 and over. Similarly, the lifelong learning sector (LLS) encompasses all post-compulsory education regardless of where it occurs, whereas FE generally refers to post-compulsory education that takes place within a college environment. It is really only since 2007 and the implementation of the Lifelong Learning UK (LLUK) (2007) initial teacher training standards that the term LLS became common parlance for those involved in post-16 (or, as relevant, post-14) education and training. Therefore the literature, policies and reports use the terms post-compulsory, FE and LLS interchangeably. In the most recent documentation, the name has again changed and the sector is now known as the further education and skills sector. For ease and brevity, this book will use the term FE throughout.

Similarly, differences in the names given to teacher training provision within FE also exist. These include initial teacher training (ITT), initial teacher education (ITE) and post-compulsory education and training (PCET). Again for ease and brevity, this book will use the term initial teacher training (ITT) throughout.

A SHIFTING LANDSCAPE

Variance in the sector's name and teacher training provision serves, in a limited sense, to illustrate the complexity of a sector which is constantly shifting and shaping according to changes in government ideologies, policies, reports and learners' needs. A list of reports that have been pivotal to changes within FE can be seen in Table I. I.

Table I.I Key documents and reports

Date	Title	Comments
1944	Butler Act (1944) (National Archives Cabinet Papers, 2013)	This Act introduced a tripartite system of secondary education, ie grammar, secondary modern and technical schools
1944	McNair Report (1944) (HMSO)	This report followed the Butler Act (1944) and raised concerns about deficiencies in the system of recruiting and training teachers, particularly those involved in teaching post-compulsory education
1957	Willis Jackson Report (1957) (HMSO)	Promoted the concept of a qualified post-compulsory workforce
1966	Russell Report (1966) (DES)	Continued to build on the concept of a qualified post-compulsory workforce
1972	James Report (National Archives Cabinet Papers, 2013)	Promoted post-compulsory teacher training being accredited by universities
1992	Further and Higher Education Act (Legislation.gov.uk, 2013)	Transferred responsibility for funding and governing post-compulsory education from LEAs to the FEFC, leading to a more economic, cost-efficient and 'for profit' approach
1997	Kennedy: *Learning Works* report (Kennedy, 1997)	Helena Kennedy produced this report promoting the need for colleges to offer programmes to a diverse range of learners
1998	*The Learning Age: A Renaissance for a New Britain* (Blunkett, 1998)	The Secretary of State for Education and Employment proposed the implementation of a further education national training organisation (FENTO) by the end of the year
2002	*Success For All* report (DfES, 2002)	The first of several reports suggesting that post-compulsory teacher training be reviewed and that properly trained teachers could improve the UK's workforce and economic prospects
2003	The Initial Teacher Training of Further Education Teachers (HMI 1762) (Ofsted, 2003)	The report concluded that FENTO provided a good baseline of what was required of teachers but lacked any ethos of professional development
2004	*Equipping Our Teachers for the Future* (DfES, 2004)	This report noted that training beyond qualified teaching status was necessary in order for teachers to be up to date with learners' needs
2005	Foster Report, *Realising the Potential* (Foster, 2005)	Stressed the need to address the issues of an ageing workforce and the need to improve vocational and pedagogic skills through comprehensive workforce planning

Date	Title	Comments
2006	*Raising Skills, Improving Life Chances* (DfES, 2006)	Considered that the UK's economic future depended on productivity as a nation and that the FE sector was central to achieving this but was not currently achieving its full potential as the powerhouse of a high-skills economy
Dec 2006	*Prosperity for All in a Global Economy – World Class Skills* (Leitch, 2006)	Prosperity for all could be achieved through a national training programme for those teaching in the LLS
2007	LLUK standards (LLUK, 2007)	These replaced the FENTO Standards
2007	The Further Education Teachers' Qualifications (England, No 2264) (DIUS, 2007)	These regulations stipulated that all teachers working in the LLS needed to be registered with the IfL and submit evidence of qualification and annual CPD. All lecturers joining the sector after 2001 needed to become qualified within their identified role
2009	Enquiry into Teacher Training in Vocational Education (Skills Commission, 2009)	Specifically, the enquiry set out to examine whether teachers in the LLS were being trained in the skills to deliver the emerging 14–19 vocational curricula – and proposed the merger of the General Teaching Council and the IfL in order for those working within the LLS to have parity of qualifications with teachers in schools
2009	*Workforce Strategy Report* (LLUK, 2009)	Set out priorities for training teachers including the need to employ a diverse range of teachers with backgrounds and vocational skills that align with the learners that they teach
2011	Wolf Report (DfE, 2011)	This report considered how vocational education for 14- to 19-year-olds could be improved, and promoted the concept of FE teaching in schools to ensure that young people are taught by those best suited to do so
2011	Education Strategy 2020 (World Bank Group, 2011)	Impacted on the future of teacher training in order to meet its global strategic objectives as the UK would benchmark learners' performance against a variety of comparator countries
2012	Lingfield Review (Lingfield, 2012)	This report recommended the deregulation of ITT and suggested that the regulations had not made the intended impact
2012	Consultation on the Revocation of the Further Education Workforce Regulations (BIS, 2012)	A response in relation to the proposed revocation of regulatory teacher training
2013	Qualifications Guidance for awarding organisations; level Four and level Diploma in Education and Training (LSIS, 2013b)	A new framework of units and credits for initial teacher education was introduced.
2014	The Education and Training Foundation	A new set of standards were rolled out.

Post-war educational development

Several post-war documents promoted the need to improve teaching within the post-compulsory sector. Ideological policies have continually influenced political, social and economic assumptions and subsequent change within post-compulsory education. Following radical post-war changes initiated by the Butler Act (1944), and the subsequent McNair Report (1944), post-compulsory education became recognised as a significant provider of education. However, the McNair Report (1944) described teaching in the post-compulsory sector as *dull* and the teaching methods *outdated*. It presented an argument for teachers within the post-compulsory sector to become qualified and for suitable teacher training courses to be delivered. These were short courses that emphasised the need for subject competence among staff rather than concentrating on pedagogy (Orr and Simmons, 2010).

Following the McNair Report (1944), the Willis Jackson Report (1957) and the Russell Report (1966) continued to promote the concept of a qualified post-compulsory workforce, although training was generally focused on skills rather than any theoretical framework, and it was not mandatory to become qualified. The Further and Higher Education Act, in April 1992, transferred the responsibility for FE colleges from Local Education Authorities (LEAs) to the Further Education Funding Council (FEFC), which in 2000 became the Learning and Skills Council (LSC) (Armitage et al., 2003), which subsequently became the Skills Funding Agency (SFA) in April 2010 (SFA, 2013). The intention of the 1992 transfer was to incorporate colleges and to give them autonomy and responsibility for growth and student recruitment. Colleges became managed by a board of governors and a senior management team. Although they were required by the government to follow national strategies, they were able to act independently according to their own specific vision, finances and strategies (Smithers and Robinson, 2000).

In 2005, Sir Andrew Foster reviewed the FE sector and subsequently issued a report, *Realising the Potential*, which stressed the need for:

values of greater clarity, improved leadership, organisation and management and a relentless focus on the needs of learners and business as the criteria for progress. (Foster, 2005, p4)

This pivotal report maintained that improvement to teaching and learning was essential for the success, achievement and retention of learners and for the growth of the economy. This view was also borne out in a White Paper *Raising Skills, Improving Life Chances* (2006), in which Tony Blair (then Prime Minister) purported that:

Our economic future depends on our productivity as a nation ... the colleges and training providers that make up the FE sector are central to achieving that ambition. (DfES, 2006, p3)

TEACHER TRAINING

It was several decades after the Butler Act (1944) and McNair Report (1944) that the James Report (1972) emerged (Table I.I). This report emphasised the need for post-compulsory teacher training and similarly, five years later in 2007, so did the Hodgson Report (Armitage et al., 2003).

It was several years after these reports that a Green Paper, *The Learning Age* (Blunkett, 1998), recommended the implementation of a further education national training organisation (FENTO) to oversee and endorse teacher training qualifications. Underpinning these endorsed teaching qualifications were a set of standards which FENTO rolled out in 2001. The intention of these standards was to raise the quality of teaching in order to improve learners' achievement and retention.

A regulated sector

Although FENTO regulated that all new teachers (post-2001) needed to become qualified, the *arrangements for initial teacher training varied enormously between colleges and between different subject areas* (Lucas, 2004, p36). Subsequently, and following a series of further government reports (DfES, 2004, 2006; Foster, 2005; Leitch, 2006 – see Table I.I), FENTO was replaced, in 2005, by Lifelong Learning UK (LLUK). In 2007, LLUK issued a new set of standards, and from then, until 2012, it became compulsory for all teachers within the sector to become qualified.

The LLUK (2007) standards contained core units of assessment within a 120-credit framework (Lingfield, 2012). These standards were designed with the intention of providing a benchmark of the skills and attributes required by trainees in order for them to become qualified (DfES, 2004). As reported by the Skills Commission (2009, p4), education within FE could only be as good as those teaching within it and a qualified workforce would improve the achievement of learners and enable them to work and to compete in a globalised economy and working environment. This was all the more urgent because of the expected growth in the number of trainees from a variety of vocational areas due to *the statutory education leaving age rising to 18 in 2015* (Skills Commission, 2009, p27).

Teaching qualifications available to teachers from 2007 were:

○ Preparing to Teach in the Lifelong Learning Sector (PTLLS) – levels 3 or 4;

○ Certificate in Teaching in the Lifelong Learning Sector (CTLLS) – levels 3 or 4;

○ Diploma in Teaching in the Lifelong Learning Sector (DTLLS) – level 5;

○ Standalone diplomas in Teaching English (Literacy) in the Lifelong Learning Sector, Teaching English (ESOL) in the Lifelong Learning Sector, Teaching Mathematics (Numeracy) in the Lifelong Learning Sector – level 5;

○ Integrated diplomas in Teaching English (Literacy) in the Lifelong Learning Sector, Teaching English (ESOL) in the Lifelong Learning Sector, Teaching Mathematics (Numeracy) in the Lifelong Learning Sector – level 5.

Additionally, some higher education institutions (HEIs) offered:

○ Certificate in Education in the Lifelong Learning Sector (Cert.Ed) – level 5 – equivalent to the DTLLS level 5 qualification;

o Professional Graduate Certificate in Teaching in the Lifelong Learning Sector (PGCE) – level 6;

o Postgraduate Certificate in Teaching in the Lifelong Learning Sector (PGCE) – level 7.

In order to become qualified within FE, trainees needed to achieve a PTLLS qualification, which provided them with an initial licence to practise, followed by attainment of either a CTLLS or DTLLS qualification. Some universities validated these qualifications using different titles, for example, Certificate or Diploma in Education. Whether a trainee enrolled onto a CTLLS or a DTLLS initial teacher training qualification was dependent upon their job role and teaching responsibilities, as stipulated by the LLUK (2007) standards. CTLLS was seen to be suitable for teachers who did not have a full teaching role. These teachers were seen as Associate Lecturers and, upon completion and achievement of the CTLLS qualification, they could apply for Associate Teacher of Learning and Skills (ATLS) status. The DTLLS qualification was seen as suitable for teachers who had a full teaching role. These teachers, upon completion and achievement of the DTLLS qualification, could apply for Qualified Teacher of Learning and Skills (QTLS) status.

Additionally, in order to achieve ATLS or QTLS status, teachers needed to undertake a minimum of 30 hours (pro-rata if they were part time) professional development and to be registered with the Institute for Learning (IfL). This requirement complied with the Further Education Teachers' Continuing Professional Development and Registration (England) Regulations (2007, p3), which stipulated compulsory registration and continuing professional development (CPD) for all teachers by March 2008 (2007, p3). These regulations were seen by the IfL (2009, p5) to *provide a professional, flexible and responsive approach that took account of its members diversity.* It was considered very important to have trainees and teachers from varied subject disciplines due to the range of learners and subjects delivered in the sector. A report, *Equipping Our Teachers for the Future*, contends that the quality of teaching affects the achievements and life chances of *about six million learners annually in the LLS* (DfES, 2004, p5).

The rationale behind the implementation of a regulatory initial teacher training qualification emerged from the Labour government's (1997–2010) belief that improvement to the teaching and learning provision within FE was necessary for the development of a *world-leading education system that would be at the heart of national priorities for economy and society* (DIUS, 2007, p2). It was the function of the LSC (established by the Labour government in 2000 and replaced by the SFA in 2010) to ensure that high-quality post-16 provision was available to *meet the needs of employers, individuals and communities* (DfEE, 1999, p23). With this mandate and with post-compulsory education being profiled as providing an opportunity for widening participation, the gaining of qualified teacher status became increasingly important to those spearheading these initiatives.

Changes to the sector following the Lingfield (2012) review

A result of having so many policies, a diverse workforce and a tiered initial teacher training model within FE was that initial teacher training became seen as being *over-complicated*

(Lingfield, 2012, p7). In September 2012, as a result of amended *workforce regulations* (LSIS, 2013a, p4), it was no longer mandatory for teachers working within FE to be members of the IfL or to work towards professionalisation and QTLS status. This *signalled a new approach that did not need to rely upon government regulation but rather gave the sector some autonomy to decide for itself the best way to raise, and to maintain, standards* (LSIS, 2013a, p4). LSIS was tasked with *reviewing, renaming and simplifying the teaching qualifications* (LSIS, 2013a, p5) and from this, and within the Qualifications and Credit Framework (QCF), emerged several qualifications, some of which are outlined later in this book in Chapter 9. (There is also a link to further reading about these at the end of this introductory chapter.) One of these qualifications was the level 4 CET qualification. From March 2013 LLUK was replaced by LSIS, which, later in 2013, was replaced by the Education and Training Foundation (ETF).

WHAT IS THE LEVEL 4 CERTIFICATE IN EDUCATION AND TRAINING QUALIFICATION?

From September 2013, it became the responsibility of employers to decide what qualifications were most appropriate for their staff (LSIS, 2013a). Although the CTLLS qualification, which will ceased to exist in 2014, and the new CET qualification have similarities, they also have differences. For example, both qualifications focus on the development of practical skills and both are, according to the QCF, level 4 qualifications. The level of a qualification is determined by its *level of difficulty and the standards of knowledge, skills and competence* that are required, and they range from *entry level to level 8* (Ofqual, 2013, p1). The CTLLS qualification was made up of 24 credits and could be completed at either level 3 or level 4. It was intended for teachers who did not have a full teaching role, as defined by the (now defunct) LLUK (2007) guidance document. The CET qualification is intended for those who:

○   want a qualification that focuses on practical teaching;

○   want a wide choice of optional units to reflect the context in which they teach;

○   are currently teaching and want to have their experience and practice accredited;

○   can meet the minimum practice requirement of 30 hours but are currently not teaching;

○   are able to undertake a qualification of a medium size;

○   have the potential to study at this level, which is the same level of demand as the first year of an undergraduate degree;

○   are willing to undertake an initial assessment of their skills in English, Mathematics and ICT, record their development needs and to follow an action plan to address them if necessary (LSIS, 2013a, p9).

The level 4 CET qualification is made up of 36 credits, with a minimum of 21 credits needing to be at level 4 or above, while the remaining 15 credits can be at levels 3, 4 or 5. One unit of credit is equal to ten notional hours of learning (Ofqual, 2013).

The 36 credits that you need to achieve in order to be accredited with a CET qualification are made up from:

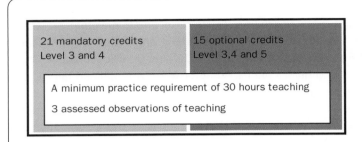

Figure I.1 Outline of the level 4 Certificate in Education and Training qualification

Source: LSIS (2013a, p10)

One of the mandatory units is at level 3. The other four are at level 4. Optional units are available at levels 3, 4 and 5.

The mandatory requirements for the level 4 CET qualification are covered in the following units.

Understanding roles, responsibilities and relationships in education and training (3 credits at level 3).

○ Planning to meet the needs of learners in education and training (3 credits at level 4).

○ Delivering education and training (6 credits at level 4).

○ Assessing learners in education and training (6 credits at level 4).

○ Using resources for education and training (3 credits at level 4).

Source: (LSIS, 2013a, p10)

Your tutor will advise you about the optional units that are available to you and which are the most appropriate for you in relation to the context in which you teach. You will find a link to further reading about the range of available optional units at the end of this introductory chapter and a list of those currently available can be found in Appendix 2.

The chapters within this book cover the range of topics that are included in these units. All of the units are underpinned by the overarching standards as outlined by the ETF and you are required to apply these standards across the units that you complete. A link to these standards can be found in the references at the end of this chapter. Running through all of the standards introduced by the ETF is the need for you to reflect and to apply reflection to your practice. Demonstrating your ability to reflect on your practice will be integral to completing the LSIS units. The first chapter of this book supp⌐ understanding, development and ability to apply reflection to your practice.

Also running through the standards is the notion of developing your Minimum Core skills.

Minimum Core

It is important that you are able to demonstrate and apply the necessary levels of knowledge, understanding and personal skills in English, numeracy and information communication technology (ICT) that are required of you as a teacher. You will find reference to these Minimum Core requirements in the LSIS units that you do with specific reference being made to them in the four, level four, mandatory units. This book supports your understanding of these Minimum Core requirements as well as your ability to develop the skills required. You will find more information about the Minimum Core requirements in Chapter 7.

Required teaching hours

As the level 4 CET qualification is about improving and developing your practical skills you will need to have at least 30 hours of teaching. This teaching can be with individuals and/or with groups. As a minimum, some (check how many with your tutor) of these 30 hours need to be allocated to the three education and training mandatory units listed below.

- Delivering education and training (6 credits at level 4).
- Assessing learners in education and training (6 credits at level 4).
- Using resources for education and training (3 credits at level 4).

Observation

At least one observation needs to take place during the coverage of each of these units and therefore it is not possible to pass any of them without some coverage of teaching hours. Specifically, Chapter 8 offers guidance about how you can prepare for your observations as well as what you can expect to happen during and after the observation process.

PROGRESSION

As well as providing guidance and support in your studies for the level 4 CET qualification and in your development as a teacher, this book, in Chapter 9, provides information about possible progression routes. This includes information about recognition of prior learning (RPL). RPL provides a pathway to use the credits gained from your CET qualification towards other qualifications, including the Diploma in Education and Training (DET) qualification.

SUMMARY

You can see from the information provided in this introduction that, as trainee teachers, you belong to a sector that has not, and does not, stand still. It is a sector that constantly strives to make a difference and to provide qualified and skilled teachers who can give their learners a quality education that will equip them with the skills, attitudes and attributes to live and to work in the society to which they belong.

 TAKING IT FURTHER

In addition to the literature already commented upon in this chapter you may find the following literature of interest.

Education and Training Foundation, (2014), http://www.et-foundation.co.uk/

Excellence Gateway, addressing literacy, language, numeracy and ICT needs in education and training. Defining the minimum core of teachers' knowledge, understanding and personal skills: www.excellencegateway.org.uk/node/12019.

REFERENCES

Armitage, A., Bryant, R., Dunnill, R., Flanagan, K., Hayes, D., Hudson, A., and Kent, J. (2003) *Working in Post-Compulsory Education*. Buckingham: Open University Press.

BIS (2012) *Consultation on the Revocation of the Further Education Workforce Regulations*. London: Department of Business, Innovation and Skills.

Blunkett, D. (1998) *The Learning Age*, Green Paper, Response Summary, www.lifelonglearning.co.uk/greenpaper/summary.pdf [accessed July 2015].

Butler Act (1944) The Cabinet Papers *1915–1982*. Retrieved 17 June 2009, The National Archives, www.nationalarchives.gov.uk/cabinetpap [accessed June 2013].

DfES (1999) *Learning To Succeed: A New Framework for Post-16 Learning*. London: HMSO.

DfES (2002) *Success For All Report: Reforming Further Education and Training*. London: DfES.

DfES (2004) *Equipping Our Teachers for the Future*. London: DfES.

DfES (2006) *Raising Skills Improving Life Chances*. London: DfES.

DIUS (2007) *The Further Education Teachers' Qualifications (England)*. London: HMSO.

Foster, A. (2005) *Realising the Potential: A Review of the Future Role of Further Education Colleges, Report Summary*. Nottingham: DfES.

Further Education Teachers' Continuing Professional Development and Registration Regulations (England) (2007), The National Archives, www.legislation.gov.uk/uksi/2007/2116/contents/made [accessed July 2015].

IfL (2006) *Towards a New Professionalism*, IfL Annual Conference. London: IfL.

IfL (2009) *Review of CPD, Making a Difference for Teachers, Trainers and Learners*. London: IfL.

Kennedy, H. (1997) *Learning Works: Widening Participation in Further Education*. Coventry: FEFC.

Leitch, S. (2006) *Leitch Review, Prosperity for All in the Global Economy – World Class Skills*, www.hm-treasury.gov.uk/leitch [accessed June 2015].

Lingfield, R. (2012) *Professionalism in Further Education, Interim Report*. London: Department for Business, Innovation and Skills.

LLUK (2007) *New Overarching Professional Standards for Teachers, Trainers and Tutors*. London: LLUK, http://www.et-foundation.co.uk/wp-content/uploads/2014/04/new-overarching-standards-for-ttt-in-lifelong-learning-sector.pdf.

LLUK (2009) *The Workforce Strategy Report for the Further Education Sector in England, 2007–2012 (revised)*. London: Lifelong Learning UK.

LSIS (2013a) *Teaching and Training Qualifications for the Further Education and Skills Sector in England: Guidance for Employees and Practitioners*, Coventry: LSIS, http://webarchive.nationalarchives.gov.uk/20130802100617/http:/lsis.org.uk/sites/www.lsis.org.uk/files/Guidance-for-Employers-and-Practitioners-2013-April.pdf [accessed June 2015].

LSIS (2013b) *Qualifications Guidance for Awarding Organisations: Level Four Certificate in Education and Training* (QCF), Coventry, LSIS, www.excellencegateway.org.uk/node/65 [accessed September 2015].

Lucas, N. (2004) The FENTO fandango: national standards, compulsory teaching qualifications and the growing regulation of FE college teachers. *Journal of Further and Higher Education*, 28(1): 35–51.

McNair Report (1944) *Report of the Committee Appointed by the President of the Board of Education to Consider the Supply, Recruitment and Training of Teachers and Youth Leaders*, London: HMSO.

Ofqual (2013) *Qualifications and Credit Framework*, www.ofqual.gov.uk/qualifications-and-assessments/qualification-frameworks/ [accessed July 2013].

Ofsted (2003) *The Initial Training of Further Education*, www.ofsted.gov.uk/Ofsted-home/Publications-and-research/Browse-all-by/Education/Teachers-and-teacher-training/Phases/Post-compulsory/The-initial-training-of-further-education-teachers-2003 [accessed July 2015].

Orr, K., and Simmons, R. (2010) Dual identities: the in-service teacher trainee experience in the English further education sector. *Journal of Vocational Education and Training*, 62(1): 75–88.

Russell Report (1966) *The Supply and Training of Teachers for Further Education*. London: Department of Education and Science.

SFA (2013) http://skillsfundingagency.bis.gov.uk/ [accessed July 2015].

Skills Commission (2009) *Skills Commission into Teacher Training in Vocational Education*. London: Skills Commission.

Smithers, A., and Robinson, P. (2000) *Further Education Re-formed, Microsoft Reader*. Microsoft.

Willis Jackson Report, Ministry of Education (1957) *The Supply and Training of Teachers in Technical Colleges*. London: HMSO.

Wolf, A. (2011) *Review of Vocational Education*. London: Department for Education, https://www.gov.uk/government/publications/review-of-vocational-education-the-wolf-report [accessed July 2015].

World Bank Group (2011) *Learning for All: Investing in People's Knowledge and Skills, World Bank Group Education Strategy, 2020*. Geneva: World Bank.

Reflecting, evaluating and improving your practice

What is meant by critical reflection and evaluation of practice?

Theories and models of reflection

Who should reflect?

Assumptions and espoused theories

Why should you reflect?

Reflecting, evaluating and improving your practice

Where should you reflect?

How can you reflect?

Kolb's experiential learning cycle

When should you reflect?

Brookfield's four lenses

What should you do with all this reflection?

KEY WORDS

action, application, critical reflection, development, evaluation, espoused theories, in-action learning, learners, meta-cognition, on-action model, practice, prospective, teachers, thinking.

PROFESSIONAL LINKS

Throughout your course, as well as in your career as a teacher, it is important for you to develop your ability to reflect and to be a reflective enquirer. Reflecting and applying reflection to your practice underpins all of the) 20 standards outlined by the Education and Training Foundation (ETF) (2014). ETF introduce these standards by noting that

Teachers and trainers are **reflective** *and* **enquiring** *practitioners who think* **critically** *about their own educational assumptions, values and practice in the context of a changing contemporary and educational world.*

Specifically, this chapter also contributes to the following Professional Standards as provided by the Education and Training Foundation (ETF) (2014):

Professional values and attributes

Develop your own judgement of what works and does not work in your teaching and training.

1 Reflect on what works best in your teaching and learning to meet the diverse needs of learners.

2 Evaluate and challenge your practice, values and beliefs.

10 Evaluate your practice with others and assess its impact on learning.

A list of all of the Standards can be found at the back of this book (Appendix 1).

INTRODUCTION

This chapter provides a theoretical appreciation of what it means to be a reflective practitioner and it asks questions and contains activities that are designed to develop your understanding of how to apply reflection to your practice. In this way this chapter aims to meet the following objectives:

○   to provide you with an explanation of some of the key theories and models of reflection;

○   to support your exploration of ways in which you might use feedback from learners and others in order to improve your practice;

○   to assist you in identifying areas for your continual professional development.

STARTING POINT

What do you already know about reflection?

○ What do you understand by the term *reflective practice*?

○ What do you understand by the term *critically reflective practice*?

As a trainee teacher working in the Further Education and Skills sector you will often reflect about an event that has occurred or an action that you have taken. However, how useful any act of reflection is to you depends upon the action that you take following that reflection. Ghaye (2011, p130) cites Freire (1972), who considers that

reflection without action is just wishful thinking.

WHAT IS MEANT BY CRITICAL REFLECTION AND EVALUATION OF PRACTICE?

Critically reflecting is linked to your ability to think critically; that is to make logical connections between ideas that subsequently support your evaluation of facts and opinions in order to make a sound judgement of an event, action or encounter. Using and developing the necessary skills for reflection are pivotal to your development as a professional practitioner as you will regularly need to reflect about:

○ what it is you are doing;

○ why you are doing it;

○ what you need do differently next time.

Reflecting critically about experiences that have occurred in your practice as well as acknowledging the feelings that you have in relation to them enables *new* thinking and *new* ideas to be formed and it is these *new* concepts that allow *new* experiences to occur (Gibbs, 1998).

THEORIES AND MODELS OF REFLECTION

There is a wealth of literature available that provides information about what reflection and reflective practice is. Much of this information has been developed from established theories and models of reflection. Some of the most significant theories are outlined in Table 1.1 below.

You will find it useful to read literature relating to all of the models presented in Table 1.1, several of which are discussed in more detail in the following sections.

Table 1.1 Reflective practice: examples of some of the key theorists

Theorist	Year	Characteristics of model
Jennifer Moon	2006	Progression from description to more critical reflection of events
Donald Schön	2002	Reflecting in action and on action
Johns	1995	Using a framework of five cue questions
Gibbs	1998	Learning by doing
Stephen Brookfield	1985	Reflecting through four different lenses
David Kolb	1984	Cyclical experiential learning model
Donald Schön and Chris Argryis	1978	Single and double loop learning
John Dewey	1933	Active, persistent, and careful consideration of any belief or knowledge; challenging those beliefs and knowledge

Within education, reflective practice relates to the application of the skill of reflection around the *process of learning and the representation of that learning* in order to improve professional practice (Moon, 2006, p4). All of the three types of reflection (prospective, in action and on action) are central to effective pedagogic practice (Moon, 2006, p4).

Prospective reflection is an active, persistent and careful consideration of any belief or practice in light of its current position and possible eventual consequences (Dewey, 1933, cited in Han, 1995, p1). In essence, this is pre-flection and means thinking before an action is taken about its possible consequences. For example, if you were going to use some new, or different, technology during a lesson, you might consider the consequences that this might have on the learners' learning experiences if the technology did not work or was not as successful as you intended it to be.

Question

What skills might you need to complete and achieve the level 4 CET qualification?

Answer

Possible answers could include whether your current literacy, presentation and ICT skills are going to be sufficient to meet the requirements of the course. Not having sufficient skills could impact upon your achievement, therefore giving some thought about how you could develop these skills would be useful. You might find it useful to write down and analyse your strengths, weaknesses, opportunities and threats. Doing this is called a SWOT analysis; you will find more details about this in Chapter 9.

Reflection in action refers to a person's (teacher's) need to examine their prior understanding of theories in use and to construct new understandings when presented with a *unique situation* while in the classroom (Schön, 2002, p130). Theories in use refer to those theories (even those that you may have forgotten about) that over the course of time have influenced your attitudes and your beliefs and these, in turn, will have influenced your actions and responses to an event. Put more simply, reflection in action is the action of *thinking on your feet* and reflecting on something while you are actually doing it. Doing this can result in an instant decision being made that can result in a change of action in relation to how you are approaching a task or situation. For example, if a lesson that you have planned is going badly you might, midway through the lesson, decide to do something very different from what you had planned. During reflection in action you might consciously or unconsciously draw upon theories that you have learned during your teacher training or through prior learning. For example, you might draw upon theories relating to behaviour management techniques that might encourage learners to engage more actively in the lesson.

Reflection on action refers to the act of reflecting on your action/s after the event, ie taking the chance to reflect following an experience (Schön, 2002, p279). Put simply, this is *thinking following* an event or action taken. For example, after you have had a teaching observation you may reflect about the strengths of the lesson and what you consider to be the areas for future development. Indeed, very often the observer will ask you to comment and to provide your views about the lesson.

WHY SHOULD YOU REFLECT?

Among others, Moon (2006), as well as Huddleston and Unwin (2002), stresses that it is a person's use of mental models to explore and examine theories in use that influence their responses during their process and application of reflection, which can ultimately lead to changes in attitudes and outcomes. Action in the sense of reflection does not relate purely to physical activity; it also applies to any action you take relating to your mental models. For example, through reflection you may realise that you need to change your assumptions or to look at a problem differently (Brookfield, 1995). The action relates to your shift in thinking which will ultimately influence a possible change in your behaviour or your approach to future incidents. Therefore, continually reviewing and developing your mental models is important in order for you to make informed decisions that lead to improved outcomes and strategies. Therefore reflection is important in order to:

○ review an event that has occurred or action that you have taken;

○ consider the outcome and consequence of an event and/or action;

○ consider your reaction to an unforeseen event and how you might address a similar action in future (for example, dealing with unforeseen behaviour by a learner);

○ consider something that you have learned, maybe some theory or a skill, and how you could use this theory or develop this skill in the future;

○ review something that you have observed in order to consider what, if anything, you would do differently next time (for example, something observed during an observation of a peer);

○ consider personal and professional development needs and to develop a plan of action.

Question

Have you reflected on the learning that you have gained from any professional development activity that you have undertaken recently?

Answer

Reflections about a recent professional development activity might include thoughts about how, and why, the activity has changed some element of your practice, your thinking or has added to your knowledge and understanding of your practice. From these *on-action* (Schön, 2002) reflections you could consider and then plan how you would do something differently within your practice or your ongoing training in the future.

WHO SHOULD REFLECT?

Everyone should reflect. Reflection can be an individual action or a group action depending upon the reason/s for reflection. For example, you may reflect following each of your teaching lessons, or it may benefit the whole team to reflect about how well a module has been received by the learners, as well as reflecting about how it could be improved the next time that it is delivered.

Question

Is it just in educational environments that reflective practice is encouraged?

Answer

No, many professions encourage the act and application of reflection in order to improve practice, for example, the nursing and legal professions promote the use of reflective practice within their training structures.

HOW CAN YOU REFLECT?

Among others, Kolb (1984) and Brookfield (1995) provide models that can be used to enhance your ability to reflect and it is useful to read what they, as well as other theorists that you may come across, have to say about the various strategies that you could use in order to apply reflection to your practice.

Brookfield's four lenses

Specifically, Brookfield (1995, p30) suggests that a good approach to critical reflection is to look through four different lenses.

Brookfield's (1995) four lenses:

1. autobiographical as both learner and teacher;

2. seeing ourselves through our learners' eyes;

3. seeing ourselves through our colleagues' eyes;

4. theoretical literature.

Autobiographical lens as a learner and teacher

Looking at yourself through an autobiographical lens refers to your engagement in the process of self-reflection as both a teacher and a learner. As you do this you can become more aware of any assumptions that you hold and the instinctive thoughts that frame what you say and how you work. When you know what these are you can start to test their accuracy and validity *through conversations with your learners, colleagues, peers and by reading literature* (Brookfield, 1995, p30). However, challenging your assumptions can be a really difficult thing to do. Not only may you not be aware of them but you may not want to let go of something that you have thought true for most of your life. Examples of some assumptions include:

○   all adults are motivated learners;

○   adults who have vocational skills are not as clever as adults with academic skills;

○   teachers should know all of the answers to the subjects that they teach;

○   once group work has been set teachers should always interact with the groups.

One way of developing your ability to self-assess and to become more aware of any assumptions might be through keeping a diary, journal or log of critical incidents. Although these are often used as a resource to record descriptions of events, they can, particularly with practice, be used as a resource to record reflective accounts about critical incidents. These accounts become reflective when, rather than simply describing an event or action, you think about a critical incident and learn from it.

A critical incident is something that is important to you. It is often something that was unforeseen and that you have dealt with by *thinking on your feet,* or, as Schön (2002) comments, when you have reflected in action. When writing about a critical incident you need to consider:

○   the context of the incident;

○   why the incident was significant;

○   why you acted in the way that you did;

○   what skills you used and what theories you applied;

○   what you would do differently next time.

Your learners' eyes

This relates to the ways that you, as a teacher, can find ways to see yourself through your learners' eyes. This might be through the learners' evaluations of the classes that you teach and that they attend or by talking with the learners. It may even be by trying (imaginatively) to put yourself in a learner's place. Looking at your practice through your learners' eyes can help you to *check whether learners take the meanings that you intend from your teaching lessons* (Brookfield, 1995, p30).

Question

What systems and processes do you use in order to receive feedback about your teaching lessons from your learners?

Answer

Answers could include: online learner feedback questionnaires, post-lesson feedback, learner/staff meetings, module feedback, organisational learner surveys.

Your colleagues' eyes

This refers to engaging in critical conversation with your colleagues and peers or perhaps asking them to observe your practice and to provide you with feedback. According to Brookfield (1995, p30), colleagues and peers can often see *aspects of our practice that might be hidden from us*. Therefore colleagues and peers provide constructive feedback which can enable you to see your practice differently or cause you to reflect on possible assumptions (Brookfield, 1995). This can be a very useful process to adopt and it could be used for prospective reflection in order to inform your decisions about a future action, ie when you are pre-flecting about what action to take and what the consequences of the action might be. It can also be useful to speak with colleagues or peers after an event or action (reflection on action) as they can help you to determine if what you did was right, what you might have done, and what you could do next time.

Question

How often do you have learning conversations (a conversation with a learning purpose) with your colleagues that, within a safe and constructive environment, allow for critical discussion of practice to take place?

Answer

A learning conversation could be a scheduled meeting about a specific task/s, or a conversation with another colleague about how to plan for forthcoming teaching and learning lessons. Importantly, it should be task focused and purposeful.

Theoretical literature

This refers to giving consideration to the theories that you have read. Such literatu.
help you to understand your experiences by naming them in different ways and by providing you with some tools to change your approach to an event or actions (Brookfield,
1995). Taking notes and applying the theories to your practice can help you to become a
better practitioner through improving your decision making so that you can take appropriate action.

Question

What literature have you read that relates to the application of reflection to
practice?

Answer

Answers could include anything from the wealth of literature available about
reflective practice. (There is a suggested reading list at the end of this chapter.)

Kolb's experiential learning cycle

As can be seen in Table 1.2 Kolb (1984) outlines four significant stages of reflection.

Table 1.2 Kolb's experiential learning cycle

Concrete experience	Doing something and/or having an experience
Reflecting	Reflecting about the concrete experience and considering what happened, why it happened and what you might do differently next time
Abstract conceptualisation	Formulating your learning and conclusions that you arrive at following the reflective process about the original experience so that you can have a different type of experience than you did at the start of this process (i.e., the concrete experience)
Active experimentation	Testing out your newly formed ideas when the opportunity presents itself to do so

Question

How do models of reflective practice assist you when you are reflecting?

Answer

Models provide a structure and possible strategy around the process of reflection.

ASSUMPTIONS AND ESPOUSED THEORIES

As noted earlier in this chapter, Schön (2002) contends that theories in use are those theories that you consciously or unconsciously refer to when you are engaged in or are reflecting upon an action. It is these theories that inform your thinking and assumptions. Schön also refers to espoused theories, which are those that you (like all of us) may sometimes convince yourself, or hope to convince others, that you use, but in reality you do not. Therefore espoused theories relate to the image that you are trying to convey or that you believe to be true. Critical reflection of both theories in use and espoused theories is necessary in order for you to challenge your assumptions and to change, where necessary, your mental models. However, in order to begin to think differently it is necessary to consider the process of meta-cognition.

Meta-cognition refers to the process of thinking and it involves looking inwards in order to consider the assumptions and theories in use that you have and that are influencing your thinking. As Hillier (2005) asserts:

when we reflect, we not only challenge our assumptions about why we do what we do, we can also help ourselves identify where we feel lacking and why we may be setting ourselves unnecessarily unachievable standards. (p7)

Assumptions may be so embedded (from childhood and prior learning) that they are no longer recognised as assumptions but rather are seen as facts or truths. The process of reading a range of literature, speaking with colleagues and opening your mind to alternative ways of thinking can be useful actions to take in order for you to become more aware of any assumptions that you hold. You do not necessarily need to change these assumptions (depending upon what they are) but you do need to know why you have them and, when necessary, be able to defend their appropriateness.

WHERE SHOULD YOU REFLECT?

Where you should reflect is entirely dependent upon you. At times you will reflect in situ, ie where the event is taking place. At other times you might reflect in the staffroom, as you make your way home, at home, or at other venues when you are with friends and colleagues. Generally, there is no right or wrong place in which to engage in reflection; however, it should be conducive to concentration and thinking time.

WHEN SHOULD YOU REFLECT?

Reflection mostly takes place after a critical incident has occurred. This could be either a positive or negative incident, although very often it is the latter that creates a cause and reason for reflection. It is good practice to reflect when you are planning your lessons. For example, what do you intend the response to be and what, if you look at your plans through your learners' eyes is the response and level of engagement by your learners likely to be? Similarly, it is good practice, if and when possible, to reflect following each teaching lesson. This can be especially useful if you have the opportunity to discuss the lesson with colleagues or have time to consider the lesson with regard to any re literature that you have read. There will be times when you reflect in action, wh make an instant decision to amend or change your plans or to perhaps intervene in an incident. The consistent application of reflection to practice will develop your ability to make appropriate decisions and to take appropriate actions.

WHAT SHOULD YOU DO WITH ALL THIS REFLECTION?

As noted at the beginning of this chapter, *reflection without action is just wishful thinking* (Freire, 1972, cited in Ghaye, 2011, p130). If the time that you spend engaging in reflection does not result in an action then often no benefit will have been gained from the process of reflection. Of course, there are times when you will affirm, through reflection, that your actions were correct and that you would take the same approach in the same situation next time. When this happens, the act of reflection reinforces positive behaviour and you will be more likely to respond in the same way the next time a similar incident occurs. The application of reflection to practice is crucial in order to reinforce the appropriateness of an action or for change to occur.

While it is important to reflect, it is also important to recognise that there are different levels of reflection and, at different times and for different reasons, all of these levels of reflection are valuable. Hatton and Smith (1995) refer to four levels.

- ○ *Descriptive writing* is an account of an event or action that has little or no analysis or reflection within it. It is the action of recalling the event that may serve to provide a limited and superficial level of reflection, ie cause you to deliberate about what actually happened. This approach may be used, for example, if you needed to provide an account to your manager or to another colleague about a simple event or action that had occurred during one of your lessons.

- ○ *Descriptive reflection* is an account of an event that has some consideration of the reasons the event happened in the way it did. It is still largely descriptive with no real evidence of alternative viewpoints. This approach could support, at a superficial level, any decision or change that you make to your practice.

- ○ *Dialogic reflection* is an approach in which you consider your own role and position in an event. With this approach you would consider, as objectively as possible, alternative approaches and what you might do differently next time.

- ○ *Critical reflection* is an objective and holistic view of an event. When using this approach you would consider an event in relation to your own assumptions and viewpoints. You would also take into consideration the viewpoints of other people involved in the event as well as any other influencing factors.

All reflection is important and can be used to inform action. However, critical reflection is much more than a superficial engagement in the process. Critical reflection involves your active and purposeful consideration of an issue and from this should emerge some thoughts about what (if any) action needs to be taken – in other words, a plan.

Question

What can you do to develop your skills as a critically reflective practitioner?

Answer

Critical reflection occurs when you challenge your own assumptions, biases and beliefs. You should question your reasons for doing things and you should seek out the opinions of others (through literature and/or conversation) in order to inform your actions. You should also ask yourself questions, for example:

o   what worked well?

o   why did it work well?

o   what did not work well?

o   why did it not work well?

o   how can I do things differently next time?

If you do not reflect upon your experiences you are likely to continue having the same type of experiences and, as Brookfield (1995) says, *length of experience does not automatically confer wisdom* (p6). Reflecting on your experiences and your actions can help you to make new meanings from your new learning. Mezirow (1991) terms this *transformative learning* (p5) and this informs what and how changes can be made to your practice in order to develop more fully and to be equipped with the skills to offer a quality learning experience to your learners.

SUMMARY

As a practitioner engaged in continually developing your own practice and others' learning, it is important to engage in reflective practice and to adopt a critical stance when reading or listening to others. You need to make your own informed decisions, and critical reflection forms a crucial part in your ability to do this well. Developing your ability to critically reflect through self-assessment, learning conversations and literature not only enhances your potential to become, or remain, an outstanding practitioner but it can also enhance your ability to engage in debate and discussion at the different levels that are often expected of you as a teacher (with parents, governors, management and at conferences and events). Whatever theories you read or refer to, or whatever model of reflection you choose, you may find it useful to recall the *six wise men* to which Rudyard Kipling (1865–1936) referred:

> *I keep six honest serving-men: (They taught me all I knew)*
> *Their names are What and Where and When*
> *And How and Why and Who*

Check your understanding

You will find suggested answers to some of these questions at the back of this book.

Activity 1:   Write one sentence that defines reflection.

Activity 2:   What are the benefits of engaging in reflection?

Activity 3:   What do we mean when we refer to critically reflective practice?

Activity 4:   Think about a critical incident, maybe a class that went better or worse than you expected, or perhaps some feedback that you have received from your tutor about a recent observation or assignment that you have completed. Reflect on this incident and consider what you may do differently the next time similar circumstances occur.

Activity 5:   Consider the following classroom situations:

- ○   you felt in control of the lesson and all learners were well behaved;
- ○   you felt out of control of the lesson and you could tell that some learners were not fully engaged;
- ○   the lesson went badly.

For each situation identify the following:

- ○   what type of classroom environment was it (eg workshop, classroom, computer suite)?
- ○   how many learners (if any) were involved?
- ○   did you expect the lesson to turn out the way it did, and why?
- ○   what (if any) was the particular incident that occurred?
- ○   what impact did this have on the lesson (make it better/worse)?
- ○   what did you do at the time?
- ○   what could you do differently next time?

Activity 6:   Consider a recent incident that has occurred in your classroom and look at it from as many different perspectives as possible. For example, as well as looking at it from your own perspective, look at it from your learners' and colleagues' point of view and try to take account of some of the theories that have been included in this chapter or that you have read at other times. Do you think that others would look at the incident in the same way as you did?

Activity 7:   Recall a situation in which you had to make an *instant thinking on your feet* decision or action. With a colleague or peer discuss how you came to your decision.

Activity 8:   Consider one significant incident in your practice or teacher training. Ask yourself:

- why was this so significant?

- what happened?

- what have you since done with that learning, eg have you used your new learning within your practice or built on it and developed it more fully?

Activity 9:   In order to enhance your skills as a learner and teacher think about the following:

- what areas of your practice do you want to develop, ie what are your aims?

- what are your strengths, weaknesses, opportunities and threats in relation to developing these aims?

- what is your time frame for achieving your aims?

- how will you be able to measure and/ or evaluate your level of success?

Activity 10:   Refer to the case study below. Read the learner's account of one of their observed lessons and identify their levels of reflection as defined by Hatton and Smith's (1995) levels of reflective writing.

 Case study

A learner's reflections on an observed lesson

This reflection relates to the ways in which my attitude towards formative assessment has changed when considering the design, development and adaptation of the diagnostic assessment tool used during the observation of my lesson.

Using the diagnostic assessment tool within my observation went well: the variety of activities ensured that the learners remained engaged throughout the task. Throughout the formative assessment I wanted to ensure that no learners felt unable to complete the task. I attempted to address this during the start in which all learners would complete an activity individually, but then through group discussion all learners would have a glossary of definitions to refer back to.

By allowing learners to complete the first part of the assessment as a peer exercise I wanted to encourage the learners to work with each other for peer support. The seating plan is differentiated by the levels achieved in the last term, which means peer support could be easily implemented.

When designing the assessment I also took into consideration how inclusive my formative assessment tool would be. One of the learners in the class has ADHD and would therefore be disadvantaged by having to spend the entire lesson completing a written assessment. This forced me to challenge the way I was used to completing assessments in my own education. Being used to long written assessments this is naturally what I would initially consider when setting my own learners a formative assessment. Due to wanting to ensure that no learner was disadvantaged, I was required to focus on *creation*.

I know that learners with ADHD can get distracted easily and this meant that to create a truly inclusive formative assessment activity I needed to ensure it was suitable for the range of abilities of the learners and for those learners who had a specific learning need or difficulty. From my own experience of assessments and the negativity that can be created by assessments, I knew that my assessment must align itself with the concept of inclusivity and must ensure that all learners remained motivated to learn. If incorrectly designed the assessment tool could have ostracised members of the class and could have damaged their self-esteem. Instead the aim was to nurture all the learners, giving them confidence in their ability.

In hindsight I feel that the combination of physically moving around the room during the marketplace activity and the short period of written work allowed all learners to complete the activity without being disadvantaged.

The strength of the assessment tool is that it can be reused throughout the course as it covers three of the main skills that are needed to achieve the target levels set for the learners:

- o being able to define literary devices – this was covered in the starter activity with all learners essentially creating a glossary that they could refer back to throughout the assessment;

- o identifying literary features in a text – this was completed during the marketplace activity with peer support available for learners throughout;

- o writing analytically about the writer's craft – this was the final part of the assessment. Providing learners with the mark scheme allowed learners to aim for their target level, which had been written in the front of their exercise books so all learners were aware of this.

To adapt this assessment for other classes or ability groups then the pitch of the lesson could be changed – looking for more simple literary techniques such as similes and metaphors rather than onomatopoeia and hyperbole – and a different mark scheme could be provided.

One section of the assessment that I am unsure about is the final part. Learners self-assess their work using the marking criteria. My only concern with this method is that learners who feel that they are less able than others may feel self-conscious about completing this part of the exercise. I have considered adapting this by having learners potentially writing this at the back of their book which I can look at when marking them.

Completing the formative assessment has been highly valuable to my development as a practitioner as I have had to put far more consideration into assessment methods that I use in my practice than I had previously. Being used to studying at university I had forgotten many of the more creative ways in which learners could be assessed as I'm more used to essay writing. This observation and assessment development has made me think more creatively about assessment.

End of chapter reflections: Outline five key points that you have learned from reading this chapter.

 TAKING IT FURTHER

In addition to the literature already commented upon in this chapter you may find the following of interest.

Appleyard, N., and Appleyard, K. (2015), *Reflective Teaching and Learning in Further Education*, Northwich, Critical Publishing

Boud, D., and Falchikov, N. (2007) *Rethinking Assessment in Higher Education: Learning for the Longer Term*. London: Routledge.

Brookfield, S. (2012) *Teaching for Critical Thinking: Tools and Techniques to Help Learners Question Their Assumptions*, San Francisco, CA: Jossey-Bass.

Developing Reflective Practice, www.internationalstaff.ac.uk/learning-and-teaching/developing-reflective-practise/ [accessed July 2015].

Hall, Hindmarch, Hoy and Machin (2015) *Supporting Primary Teaching and Learning*, Northwich: Critical Publishing

Machin, L., Hindmarch, D., Richardson, T., Murray, S., (2015) *A Complete Guide to the Level 5 Diploma in Education and Training*, 2nd edn, Northwich, Critical Publishing.

Marcus, J., Miguel, E., and Tellima, H. (2009) Teacher reflection on action: what is said (in research) and is done (in teaching). *Reflective Practice*, 10(2): 191–204.

McGregor, D., and Cartwright, L. (eds) (2011) *Developing Reflective Practice: A Guide for Beginning Teachers*. Maidenhead, Open University Press, McGraw-Hill Education.

Mezirow, J., and Associates (eds) (1990) *Fostering Critical Reflection in Adulthood*. San Francisco, CA: Jossey-Bass.

Roffey-Barentsen, J., and Malthouse, R. (2009) *Reflective Practice in the Lifelong Learning Sector*. Exeter: Learning Matters.

SWOT: www.businessballs.com/swotanalysisfreetemplate.htm [accessed July 2015].

REFERENCES

Brookfield, S. (1995) *Becoming a Critically Reflective Teacher*. San Francisco, CA: Jossey-Bass.

ETF (2014) www.et-foundation.co.uk/, [accessed May 2015].

Ghaye, T. (2011) *Teaching and Learning Through Reflective Practice, A Practical Guide for Positive Action*. Oxon: Routledge.

Hatton, N., and Smith, D. (1995) Reflection in teacher education: towards definition and implementation. *Teaching and Teacher Education*, 11(1): 33–49.

Han, E.P. (1995) Reflection is essential in teacher education. *Childhood Education*, 71(4), www.questia.com/googleScholar.qst?docId=5002225945 [accessed July 2013].

Hillier, Y. (2005) *Reflective Teaching in Further and Adult Education* (2nd edn). London: Continuum.

Huddleston, P., and Unwin, L. (2002) *Teaching and Learning in Further Education: Diversity and Change*. London: Routledge Falmer.

Kipling, R. (1902) The Elephant's Child, in *The Literature Network*, www.online-literature.com/poe/165 [accessed June 2015].

Kolb, D.A. (1984) *Experiential Learning as the Science of Learning and Development*. Englewood Cliffs, NJ: Prentice Hall.

Mezirow, J. (1991) *Transformative Dimensions of Adult Learning*. San Francisco, CA: Jossey-Bass.

Moon, J. (2006) *Reflection in Learning and Professional Development*. Oxon: Routledge Falmer.

Schön, D. (2002) *The Reflective Practitioner*. Aldershot: Ashgate.

2 Professional roles and responsibilities

Legislation and regulatory requirements

Professional codes of practice

What are your roles as a teacher?

What are your responsibilities as a teacher?

What are your rights as a teacher?

Disclosure and Barring Service (DBS)

Professionalism: understanding roles and responsibilities in education and training

The Data Protection Act (1998)

Key aspects of legislation, regulatory requirements and codes of practice

The Education Act (2011)

Maintaining a safe and supportive environment

Professional roles and responsibilities

The Equality Act (2010)

Promoting appropriate behaviour and respect for others

The Health and Safety At Work Act (1974, latest amendment 2013)

The Special Education Needs and Disability Code of Practice: 0–25 Years (DfE, 2014)

Working with other professionals to maintain a safe and supportive environment

Ofsted – the Office for Standards in Education, Children's Services and Skills

Working with other professionals

The emotional environment

The physical environment

> **KEY WORDS**
>
> behaviour, boundaries, codes of practice, CPD, diversity, equality,
> learner needs, learning environment, legislation, professionalism,
> regulation, responsibilities, rights, roles, standards.

PROFESSIONAL LINKS

As a teacher you are a professional. To do your job effectively you must be fully aware of your rights, roles and responsibilities. This chapter highlights many of the common requirements of teaching in the Further Education and Skills Sector – for brevity called FE within this book. The roles and responsibilities of teachers within FE are covered in all of the LSIS units, but are dealt with specifically in:

○ *Understanding roles, responsibilities and relationships in education and training (level 3): 1.1, 1.2, 1.3, 1.4; 2.1, 2.2; 3.1, 3.2, 3.3.*

Of the five mandatory units, this is the only one which is assessed at level 3. The other four units are at level 4. Therefore, in this chapter the questions and activities have been written with the intention of meeting the requirements for both levels 3 and 4.

Specifically, this chapter also contributes to the following Professional Standards as provided by the Education and Training Foundation (ETF) (2014):

Professional Values and Attributes

Develop your own judgement of what works and does not work in your teaching and training

6   Build positive and collaborative relationships with colleagues and learners

Professional knowledge and understanding

Develop deep and critically informed knowledge and understanding in theory and practice

7   Maintain and update knowledge of your subject and/or vocational area

11 Manage and promote positive learner behaviour

12 Understand the teaching and professional role and your responsibilities

Professional skills

Develop your expertise and skills to ensure the best outcomes for learners

14 Plan and deliver effective learning programmes for diverse groups or individuals in a safe and inclusive environment

19 Maintain and update your teaching and training expertise and vocational skills through collaboration with employers

A list of all of the Standards can be found at the back of this book (Appendix 1).

INTRODUCTION

It is your duty to keep up to date with changes in the sector, the requirements of your organisation and how these define your teaching practice. This chapter provides information, questions and activities in relation to these requirements. In this way the chapter aims to meet the following objectives:

○ to assist you in identifying what your teaching roles and responsibilities are in education and training;

○ to raise awareness of the ways to maintain a safe and secure working environment;

○ to explore the relationship between teachers and others in education and training.

STARTING POINT

What do you already know about your roles and responsibilities?

○ Outline your current duties as a teacher.

○ What do you think your roles are as a teacher?

○ What do you think your responsibilities are as a teacher?

PROFESSIONALISM: UNDERSTANDING ROLES AND RESPONSIBILITIES IN EDUCATION AND TRAINING

What are your roles as a teacher?

As a teacher, one of your main roles is to motivate your learners to develop their ability and aspiration to learn. You may read about *delivering training* and *facilitating learning*, but in reality you do much more than that. Your role is not just about teaching your subject or preparing learners for assessment. The focus of your role relates very much to inspiring your learners to change and develop their personal, social and professional skills to the best of their ability. In this respect, your ultimate aim is to enable your learners to understand how to take responsibility for their own development. You can do this by planning and preparing teaching and learning activities that take account of the needs and well-being of individual learners as well as groups of learners.

Some key aspects of your role as a teacher may be:

○ carrying out initial and/or diagnostic assessments;

○ clear communication with your learners, other professionals and stakeholders;

○ promoting appropriate behaviour and respect for others;

○ identifying and meeting individual learners' needs;

○ being aware of the support mechanisms available;

○ being organised;

○ being reflective, by learning from successes as well as mistakes.

What are your responsibilities as a teacher?

As a teacher, a primary responsibility is to ensure that learners are enrolled onto the correct course, in terms of meeting their needs, abilities and aspirations. Further to this, you need to ensure they are on the appropriate course in terms of meeting award and organisational requirements. In order to do this you will probably have responsibility for the following:

○ promoting a safe and supportive learning environment;

○ promoting equality and diversity;

○ adhering to key legislation, regulatory requirements and codes of practice;

○ modelling professional behaviour at all times to inspire your learners;

○ ensuring your own professional development;

○ contributing to a team of professionals in order to improve the experience and achievement of your learners;

○ designing or contributing to the design of the course curriculum;

○ negotiating appropriate learning targets for the group and individuals as appropriate to their needs and aspirations as well as the course aims;

○ planning learning activities based on the needs of your group and specific individual needs within the group;

○ designing or amending learning resources that are varied, appropriate to the award aims, and intellectually challenging for your learners;

○ keeping accurate records to contribute to your organisation's quality improvement strategy. This will include keeping accurate records of recruitment, retention, achievement and progression of your group, as well as evaluation of how these can be improved;

○ keeping accurate records of individual learners' progress and future needs. This is often referred to as an individual learning plan;

○ providing learners with appropriate points of referral as required.

With regard to this last point, your primary aim is to enable each learner to achieve to the best of their ability through working in a safe and supportive environment. It is therefore your responsibility to know who your learners should contact if they need any additional support or specialist information, such as for finance, health, study skills or counselling issues.

What are your rights as a teacher?

Your rights as a teacher will be set out in your employment contract. Your employer will also be subject to the Equality Act (2010), meaning that you should not be subject to discrimination, harassment or victimisation. We will look into the Equality Act later on in this chapter.

Question

What information have you been given by your institution about your roles, responsibilities and rights?

KEY ASPECTS OF LEGISLATION, REGULATORY REQUIREMENTS AND CODES OF PRACTICE

The FE sector is often seen as being in a constant state of change. Even the name and scope of the sector does not remain stable (see the Introduction). Within the last 20 years it has been referred to as: *Further Education, Learning and Skills, Lifelong Learning* and back to *Further Education* again. Its latest reincarnation is the *Further Education and Skills* sector. With higher education institutions such as universities, it has also been termed the *post-compulsory education sector* – but now learners from the age of 14 can access part, or in some cases, all, of their education within FE. As the name of the sector changes so do its legal requirements. It is therefore essential to keep up to date with developments on your legal responsibilities as a teacher because your organisation and professional role will be subject to government policy-led changing requirements.

Question

What are the boundaries between your teaching role and other professional roles?

Extend your understanding

Analyse the differences and impact on learners or clients in relation to these boundaries.

Legislation and regulatory requirements

Sources of information include:

○ the Department for Business, Innovation and Skills (BIS) – the ministry responsible for further education and skills;

- statutory bodies such as the Office for Teaching Standards in Education (Ofsted), the Equality and Human Rights Commission (EHRC) and the Health and Safety Executive (HSE);

- education supplements of national newspapers such as the *Times Educational Supplement* or the *Guardian* education section;

- professional bodies such as the Education and Training Foundation (ETF) and any organisations related to your subject;

- a teachers' union such as the University and College Union (UCU) or Association of Teachers and Lecturers (ATL).

Legislation is defined by an Act of Parliament. You probably won't need to read the original documents, but it is a good idea to keep up to date with how they affect your practice. A good way of doing this is via the statutory bodies which have been set up to try and ensure that the law is implemented. The following summarises some of the key legislation and responsible bodies which directly relate to your role. This is not an exhaustive list and it is important that you are aware of changes in governmental policy and how this affects your institution's policies and your own professional practice.

The Education Act (2011)

There have been many Acts of Parliament relating to education, the latest of which is the Education Act (2011). This has made widespread changes, from redefining approaches to discipline to the powers of government to control educational institutions.

The Equality Act (2010) (statutory body: the EHRC)

This act brings together all previous legislation relating to promoting equality into one legal act with the intention of protecting our human rights (DfE, 2013). There are *protected characteristics* which you must be aware of to help ensure that discrimination, victimisation and harassment are prevented.

Question

List the characteristics that you think are protected by the Equality Act (2010).

Answer

According to the EHRC (2013), the Act protects you from discrimination and harassment based on your *protected characteristics*. The *protected characteristics* for the further and higher education institutions provisions are:

- age;

- disability;

- gender reassignment;

- pregnancy and maternity;

○ race;

○ religion or belief;

○ sex;

○ sexual orientation.

Extend your understanding

Why is it important to have these protected characteristics?

The Equality Act aims to ensure that all learners and staff are free from:

○ discrimination (direct, indirect and arising from disability);

○ harassment;

○ victimisation.

Question

What policies does your institution have to try and prevent discrimination, harassment or victimisation of learners and staff?

Answer

Policies will incorporate, among others, the Equality Act (2010), Health and Safety at Work Act, Data Protection Act and Code of Practice and the Special Education Needs and Disability Code of Practice (2014).

The Health and Safety At Work Act (1974, latest amendment 2013) (statutory body: the HSE)

The HSE is the national independent watchdog for work-related health, safety and illness.

We often see stories in the media which run along the theme of everyday activities being banned by some, perhaps seemingly officious, bureaucrat. Yet it should be remembered that many of these *health and safety gone mad*-style stories may be biased or exaggerated. They do not necessarily reflect the value of careful adherence to guidelines; the everyday accidents prevented by sensible adherence to the guidelines rarely, if ever, make headlines.

Therefore, a major part of our professional practice is to take health and safety concerns seriously in terms of the learners for whom you are responsible, your colleagues and, of course, yourself. A key concept to remember is that health and safety is everyone's responsibility. So if you are aware of a potential issue, it is your responsibility to report it immediately and ensure that the learners are removed from potential harm.

Ofsted – the Office for Standards in Education, Children's Services and Skills

Ofsted is the body responsible for regulating education provision, including the FE sector. Your institution and your practice will be regularly inspected by them. An institution will receive one of four grades (Ofsted, 2015).

Ofsted grades

Grade 1: Outstanding

Grade 2: Good

Grade 3: Requires improvement

Grade 4: Inadequate

Should your institution gain a grade 3 or 4, it will, under the current guidelines, be a priority for reinspection and may face special measures. For more information, see Chapter 7.

Question

What Ofsted grade does your institution currently hold? Why?

The Special Education Needs and Disability Code of Practice: 0–25 Years (DfE, 2014)

The SEND Code of Practice (DfE 2014) updates the initial code from 2001. Whereas the original focused on school provision, this update is also aimed at colleges as it extends coverage to 25 year olds. The code now stresses the need to inform and involve parents/guardians/learners throughout the support process. It also emphasises multi-agency cooperation, with a combined Education, Health and Care needs assessment where necessary.

Question

How is your institution adhering to this code of practice?

The Data Protection Act (1998)

The use and storage of data by organisations is controlled by the Data Protection Act (DPA). This means that ensuring appropriate usage of information is a legal responsibility for the organisation and its employees. As a teacher, you may have to use potentially sensitive data to inform your professional practice. For example, personal information relating to a disability or special education needs will inform your approaches to planning and delivering learning.

Question

The DPA (1998) is guided by eight fundamental principles relating to how information is distributed, used and stored. What do you think these principles are?

Answer

According to the DPA (1998), information must be:

○   used fairly and lawfully;

○   used for limited, specifically stated purposes;

○   used in a way that is adequate, relevant and not excessive;

○   accurate;

○   kept for no longer than is absolutely necessary;

○   handled according to people's data protection rights;

○   kept safe and secure;

○   not transferred outside the UK without adequate protection.

Question

Considering the above, what are your professional responsibilities regarding data use?

Answer

You need to make sure that you adhere to all of the principles within the DPA.

Extend your understanding

What would you do if you lost or misplaced some data about one or more of your learners?

Answer

Immediately contact your line manager for guidance on institutional procedures.

Disclosure and Barring Service (DBS)

This body replaced the Criminal Records Bureau (CRB) and Independent Safeguarding Authority (ISA) in 2012. The purpose of the DBS is to help employers make safe recruitment decisions and prevent unsuitable people from working with vulnerable groups. Your employer should require you to complete a satisfactory DBS criminal record check prior to employment or the commencement of any duties at your institution. Your employer will also ask for regular updated checks throughout your career. As well as this, you are also legally obliged to immediately inform your employer of any changes to your record, or any issues which may bring about a change.

Professional codes of practice

Many professions have their own professional/trade organisation, such as Gas Safe, the Nursing and Midwifery Council and the Chartered Institute of Management Accountants.

Questions

- ○ How many professional/trade organisations can you think of?
- ○ What organisations relate to your subject?
- ○ What are the benefits of membership of such organisations?

Between 2007 and 2012 all new entrants to the FE sector were required to join its professional body, the Institute for Learning (IfL). In 2012 government deregulation of the sector ended mandatory requirements for teachers. This means that there is no longer a legal requirement for teachers to be a member of a professional body, possess teaching/subject specialist qualifications or evidence a commitment to professional training and updating. In place of the member funded IfL, the government now pays for a voluntary employer-led professional body, the Education and Training Foundation (ETF).

MAINTAINING A SAFE AND SUPPORTIVE ENVIRONMENT

There is no single set way to promote positive behaviour in all of your learners. There are many handbooks available which advise on different behaviour management techniques. You should research these and try any which you feel are suitable for your classes.

Promoting appropriate behaviour and respect for others

The overall principles for promoting appropriate behaviour and respect for others include the following:

o   the teacher needs to model appropriate behaviour;

o   learners need to be aware of what constitutes appropriate and inappropriate behaviour;

o   rewards and sanctions for behaviour need to be administered fairly and consistently.

Let's look at each of these principles in turn.

Modelling behaviour

No matter how difficult a class is to manage, modelling professional behaviour to our learners is the *first* thing we can always get right. This is in our control, so must be the starting point of all our approaches to managing the behaviour of our learners.

Question

Consider the impact on learners if a teacher:

o   is late to class;

o   appears unprepared and disorganised;

o   looks tired and unenthusiastic;

o   has a mobile phone which rings during class time;

o   is irritable.

Answer

A positive appearance is vital, even if it does not match your inner feelings. Showing respect for your learners includes being prepared and arriving in your classroom in good time to have the learning environment suitably ready. Keep your lessons interesting by using a range of appropriate teaching, learning and assessment strategies. Remember: promoting good behaviour begins with you modelling good behaviour. A positive and professional attitude supported by thorough preparation, resources and activities may take time to succeed in changing the behaviour of a problematic class – but the opposite approach will certainly fail.

Raising awareness of appropriate and inappropriate behaviour

When we think of behaviour, it's too easy to just think about *bad* behaviour – sometimes more politely known as *challenging* behaviour in education circles. However, remember that developing behaviour which supports learning is also about promoting responsibility, independence, creativity and social skills, such as the ability to work as a group.

Question

Do your learners have a clear understanding of your institution's behaviour policy in relation to:

○   what constitutes inappropriate behaviour;

○   the processes of how inappropriate behaviour will be dealt with;

○   the sanctions for inappropriate behaviour?

Rewards and sanctions for behaviour need to be applied fairly and consistently

Inconsistent application of sanctions for bad behaviour or rewards for good behaviour undermines the credibility of the teacher. Learners are less likely to change their behaviour if they feel unfairly treated. This relates not just to *punishments* for *bad* behaviour but also to when a teacher fails to recognise and acknowledge good work that a learner has done. Never consider a learner to be *not motivated*. All learners have interests and are motivated by something – it's just that they might not be motivated by your subject ... yet.

WORKING WITH OTHER PROFESSIONALS TO MAINTAIN A SAFE AND SUPPORTIVE ENVIRONMENT

One of the main responsibilities of an organisation and the teachers (and other staff) that they employ is to ensure that learners are supported within a safe environment.

A safe environment refers to:

○   the physical environment;

○   the emotional environment.

The physical environment

Your institution is responsible for providing learners with a physically safe environment. This means well-maintained buildings and equipment. Equipment must be used safely and under appropriate supervision, with appropriate risk assessments in place following HSE guidelines (1974, summarised in 2009). In this respect, health and safety is considered to be everyone's responsibility – if there is an issue it is your duty to report and cease to use any equipment or facility which you know to be dangerous.

Question

Who has overall responsibility for health and safety in your organisation?

How are learners taught about health and safety/emergency procedures at the beginning of the course? How is their *understanding* of these checked throughout the course?

Extend your understanding

Analyse your role in maintaining a safe working environment.

To help you with these questions, refer to your institution's codes of practice/policies and look at the HSE guidance checklists (see the *Taking It Further* section at the end of the chapter). If you teach a vocational subject, make sure you are aware of the latest guidance from the HSE and your subject area's professional body.

Remember, not only is it your legal responsibility to ensure your learners are safe, it is also your duty to report any issues to the relevant authority and ensure that learners are not exposed to unnecessary risk. Further to this, as a professional you should at all times model the latest guidance with regard to health and safety in your industry or trade if you are teaching a vocational subject.

The emotional environment

Reece and Walker (2007) cite Maslow (1962), suggesting that in order to provide the best learning environment it is important that learners feel emotionally safe and secure. Remember that it is our duty to ensure our learners are free from discrimination, harassment or victimisation (Equality Act 2010, cited in EHRC 2013).

Bullying

In order to promote equality of opportunities for all learners, a professional duty of the teacher is to contribute to the prevention of bullying in their organisation.

Question

What is bullying?

Answer

The DfE (2010) defined five essential components of bullying.

1. Intention to harm: bullying is deliberate, with the intention to cause harm. For example, friends teasing each other in a *good-natured* way is not bullying,

but a person teasing another with the intention to deliberately upset them is bullying.

2. Harmful outcome: one or more persons are hurt physically or emotionally.

3. Direct or indirect acts: bullying can involve direct aggression, such as hitting someone, as well as indirect acts, such as spreading rumours.

4. Repetition: bullying involves repeated acts of aggression. An isolated aggressive act, like a fight, is not bullying.

5. Unequal power: bullying involves the abuse of power by one or several persons who are (perceived as) more powerful, often due to their age, physical strength, or psychological resilience.

Research summarised by the Department for Education (2010) found that:

o bullying is more likely in environments where the bully believes such behaviour to be *normal*;

o bullies tend to focus on differences, often targeting learners with special education needs (SEN);

o being a victim of bullying not only causes emotional distress but may also reduce academic achievement.

Action should be considered in terms of prevention and intervention. To prevent the development of a culture of bullying, learners need to understand that difference is to be celebrated and that bullying is not tolerated, and the consequences of any such action must be clear for the perpetrator. Should any incidents occur, then intervention must be swift, proportionate and consistently follow the clear behaviour policy which the students have understood. Failure to act is not an option. Ofsted is clear that an institution's ability to meet learners' needs is dependent on how well they are able to create a safe environment for all learners, stating that inspectors evaluate how well:

teaching, learning and assessment promote equality, support diversity and tackle discrimination, victimisation, harassment, stereotyping or bullying. (Ofsted, 2015, p51)

Working with other professionals

Remember, there may be many factors outside of the classroom which could impact on learners' behaviour and their ability to learn. These, for example, could be financial, legal or related to health issues.

However, you cannot solve all of their problems – you are not a social worker, lawyer, bank manager, counsellor or doctor. You are probably not qualified for these roles and must never attempt to take them on in the misguided belief that you are helping your learners. This does not mean that we ignore such problems and only deal with academic issues.

It is your responsibility to *signpost* (direct) learners to the appropriate support service if they tell you of an issue or if you have reason to consider that there may be one.

A learner may request that an issue remains confidential before or after disclosing it. However, it is your duty to report any concern or issue to the relevant authorities. Therefore you must never promise to keep any issue confidential.

SUMMARY

It is important that at all times you remain professional and work within the boundaries of this role. Working alongside other professionals is also important as is an awareness of what their role is. Doing this supports the creation of a positive learning climate where learners can feel safe and secure, able ready and willing to learn.

 Check your understanding

You will find suggested answers to some of these questions at the back of this book.

Activity 1:   Summarise your rights, roles and responsibilities as a professional teacher in the FE sector and then consider this question:

Are there any elements of your practice that you need to change in order to carry out your teaching role and/or address the requirements more effectively?

Activity 2:   Read the EHRC guidance for FE providers on Equality Act (2010) and define the terms:

- o   discrimination (direct, indirect and arising from a disability);
- o   harassment;
- o   victimisation.

Activity 3:   Investigate:

- o   your institution's health and safety policy;
- o   any specific health and safety policy/ code/guidelines for your subject.

Activity 4:   Find your institution's Ofsted report and the latest Ofsted Common Inspection Framework for Further Education and Skills sector. Consider:

- o   how does your institution prepare to meet the requirements of Ofsted?

Activity 5:   Look on Ofsted's 'Good Practice' database for examples relating to your practice. What can you learn from these?

Activity 6:   Investigate your organisation's data protection policy.

Activity 7:   Consider the following:

- Are you a member of a professional body?
- What is the purpose of the body?
- What are your responsibilities to this organisation?
- What would be the implications for your trade or profession if it did not have such an organisation?

Activity 8:   What behaviour *should* a teacher model in class?

Activity 9:   Make a list of behaviours that you see in your class, dividing them into those which support learning and those which prevent or hinder it. Consider the impacts (beneficial and detrimental) that these behaviours have on maintaining and promoting a safe working environment.

Behaviour that supports learning	Potential impact	Behaviour that prevents learning	Potential impact

Activity 10:   Consider the following:

- What is your organisation's procedure for fault reporting?
- What emergency procedures are there?
- Review your workshop – make sure you are aware of the relevant HSE guidance. What equipment do you use in your teaching role? Are there any potential health and safety issues?
- Review your classroom – are there any potential health and safety issues? Is it suitable for all of your learners?
- Review your office – are there any potential health and safety issues? For example, is your workspace appropriate for your personal needs?

Activity 11:   Find your institution's behaviour management policy and consider how this policy is publicised to staff and to learners.

Activity 12:   What are the procedures for signposting learners towards appropriate support?

Activity 13:   What support services does your organisation provide?

End of chapter reflections: Outline five key points that you have learned from reading this chapter.

 TAKING IT FURTHER

In addition to the literature already commented upon in this chapter you may find the following literature of interest.

Avis, J., Fisher, R., and Thompson, R. (2011) *Teaching in Lifelong Learning: A Guide to Theory and Practice*. Oxford: Oxford University Press.

BIS: https://www.gov.uk/government/organisations/department-for-business-innovation-skills [accessed January 2015].

Byron, T. (2010) *Do We Have Safer Children in a Digital World?* Nottingham: DCSF http://webarchive.nationalarchives.gov.uk/20130401151715/http://www.education.gov.uk/publications/eOrderingDownload/DCSF-00290-2010.pdf [accessed January 2015].

Cowley, S. (2010) *Getting the Buggers to Behave (4th edn.)* London: Continuum International.

Dix, P. (2010) *The Essential Guide to Taking Care of Behaviour* (2nd edn). Gosport: Longman.

DfE (2011) *Good Behaviour in Schools – Checklist for Teachers* behaviour checklists: https://www.gov.uk/government/publications/good-behaviour-in-schools-checklist-for-teachers [accessed September 2014].

DfE (2014) *Special Education Needs Disability Code of Practice 0–25*. London: DfE www.gov.uk/government/publications/send-code-of-practice-0-to-25 [accessed January 2015].

DBS (2015): *About us* https://www.gov.uk/government/organisations/disclosure-and-barring-service/about [accessed January 2015].

ETF (2014) *The Education and Training Foundation* http://www.et-foundation.co.uk/ [accessed May 2015].

EHRC: http://www.equalityhumanrights.com/ [accessed January 2015].

EHRC *Further and Higher Education Providers' guidance*http://www.equalityhumanrights.com/advice-and-guidance/further-and-higher-education-providers-guidance [accessed January 2015].

Government Equalities Office (2013) *Equalities Act 2010: Guidance* https://www.gov.uk/equality-act-2010-guidance [accessed January 2015].

HSE: www.hse.gov.uk/index.htm [accessed January 2015].

HSE (2014) COSHH: www.hse.gov.uk/coshh/ [accessed January 2015].

Machin, L., Hindmarch, D., Murray, S. and Richardson, T. (2015) *A Complete Guide to the Level 5 Diploma in Education and Training* Northwich: Critical Publishing.

MoJ (2014) *Data Protection* https://www.gov.uk/data-protection [accessed January 2015].

Ofsted https://www.gov.uk/government/organisations/ofsted [accessed January 2015].

Teach Write Research: http://www.teachwriteresearch.com/ [accessed January 2015].

Wallace, S. (2015) *Teaching in Further Education – the inside story*. Northwich: Critical Publishing.

Vizard, D. (2012) *How to Manage Behaviour in Further Education* (2nd edn). London: Sage.

REFERENCES

DfE (2010) *Reducing Bullying amongst the Worst Affected*. UK: DfE, http://dera.ioe.ac.uk/10364/1/Reducing_Bullying_Amongst_the_Worst_Affected.pdf [accessed January 2015].

EHRC (2014) *Further and Higher Education Providers' Guidance* http://www.equalityhumanrights.com/advice-and-guidance/further-and-higher-education-providers-guidance [accessed January 2015].

HSE *Health and Safety at Work Act* (1974) www.hse.gov.uk/legislation/hswa.htm [accessed January 2015].

HSE (2009) Health and Safety at Work Act 1974 (Summary) www.hse.gov.uk/pubns/law.pdf [accessed January 2015].

Ofsted (2015) *Handbook for the Inspection of Further Education and Skills from 2014*, https://www.gov.uk/government/publications/handbook-for-the-inspection-of-further-education-and-skills-from-september-2012 [accessed January 2015].

Reece, I., and Walker, S. (2007) *Teaching, Training and Learning: A Practical Guide* (6th edn). Tyne and Wear: Business Education Publishers.

3 Learners and their needs

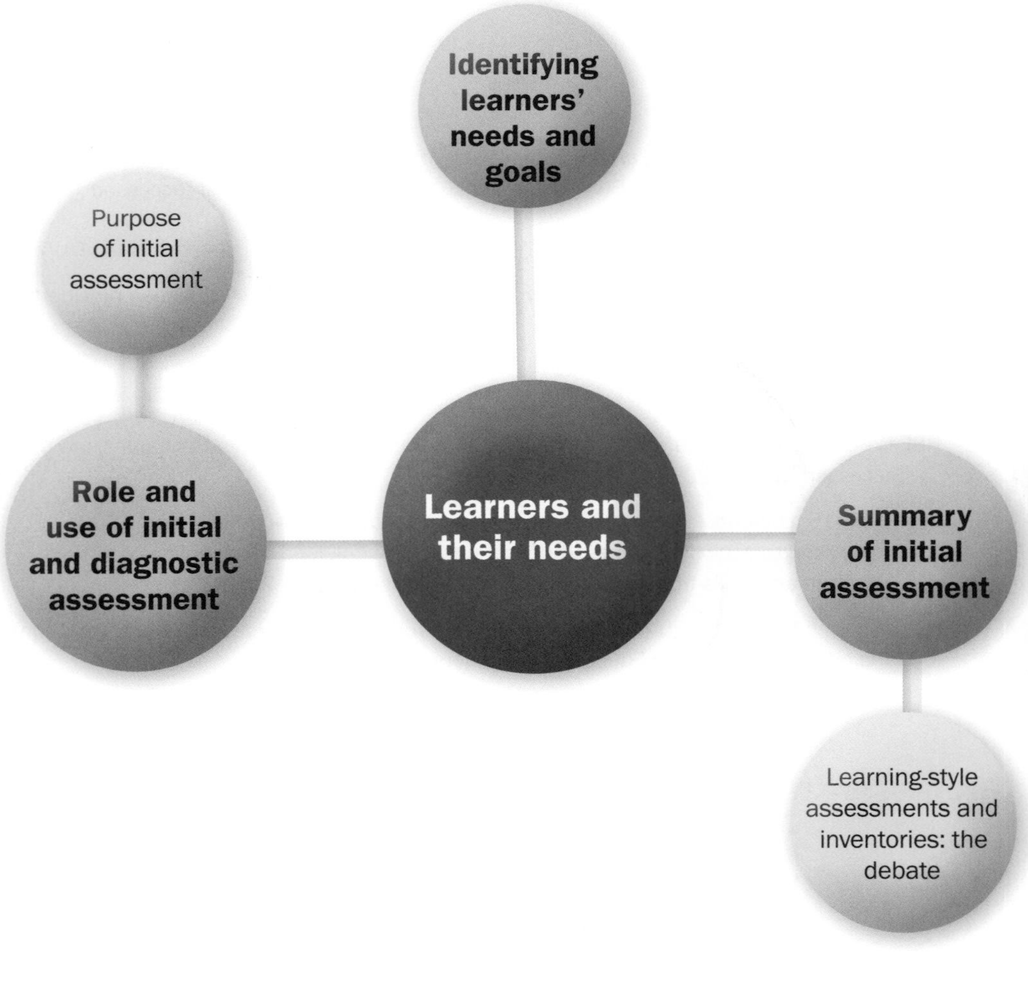

KEY WORDS

communities of learning, diagnostic assessment, equality of opportunity, goals, initial assessment, needs, planning, recruitment.

PROFESSIONAL LINKS

The focus of this chapter is to develop your ability to identify and provide for individual learner needs. Although the information provided in this chapter has relevance to many of the units within the level 4 CET qualification, it particularly covers the level 4 CET unit:

○ *Planning to meet the needs of learners in education and training (level 4): 1.1, 1.2, 1.3; 2.1, 2.2, 2.3, 2.4, 2.5; 3.1, 3.2; 4.1, 4.2.*

This chapter supports you by providing information, questions and activities relating to planning for teaching learning and assessment. It aims to meet the following objectives:

○ to be able to use initial and diagnostic assessment to agree individual learning goals with learners;

○ to be able to plan inclusive teaching and learning in accordance with internal and external requirements;

The following objective from the level 4 CET unit *Planning to meet the needs of learners in education and training* is met in Chapter 7.

○ Be able to evaluate own practice when planning inclusive teaching and learning.

Specifically, this chapter also contributes to the following Professional Standards as provided by the Education and Training Foundation (ETF) (2014):

Professional Values and Attributes

Develop your own judgement of what works and does not work in your teaching and training

5 Value and promote social and cultural diversity, equality of opportunity and inclusion

Professional knowledge and understanding

Develop deep and critically informed knowledge and understanding in theory and practice

9 Apply theoretical understanding of effective practice in teaching, learning and assessment drawing on research and other evidence

Professional skills

Develop your expertise and skills to ensure the best outcomes for learners

17 Enable learners to share responsibility for their own learning and assessment, setting goals that stretch and challenge

18 Apply appropriate and fair methods of assessment and provide constructive and timely feedback to support progression and achievement

---

STARTING POINT

Are all learners the same?

o   What do you think is meant when we use the term *learners and their needs*?

o   What do you already know about your learners? For example, do any of them have specific educational needs?

o   What are some of the similarities and differences between your learners?

ROLE AND USE OF INITIAL AND DIAGNOSTIC ASSESSMENT

The focus of diagnostic assessment is to inform both teacher and learner of the learner's current ability and future needs. In essence, initial assessment is therefore diagnostic – but it is the term which specifically refers to an assessment taken before beginning a course of learning. Further diagnostic assessments may be taken at any point during the course in order to determine changing learner needs.

Purpose of initial assessment

Initial assessment has four key aims:

1. to enrol a student onto the correct course;

2. to identify any special education needs and necessary adjustments to teaching and assessment strategies;

3. to inform learners of their current ability and future development needs;

4. to inform your planning in terms of the group and individual ability of your learners.

Aim 1: To enrol a student onto the correct course

Does the student have the right aptitude, skills and qualifications to meet the entry requirements of the course? Is there a specific English or mathematics requirement?

Your organisation and/or awarding organisation should have clear entry requirements for each course. These should be adhered to, otherwise you will be setting your learners up to fail before they have even started the course. Learners' qualifications, initial assessment details and any other required information such as DBS checks (refer to Chapter 2) need to be evidenced and recorded. This will ensure that you have evidence to demonstrate that learners are receiving appropriate advice and guidance and are being assessed as suitable for enrolment onto a course of study. These checks are important for the well-being of the learners as well as for quality assurance by bodies such as Ofsted, awarding organisations and internal/external auditors.

In their Further and Higher Education Providers' Guidance, the EHRC (2015) report that any terms that are stipulated for joining a course should not discriminate against learners:

Terms of admission should not discriminate against a person with a protected characteristic. Terms which indirectly discriminate against people with a protected characteristic or in the case of a disabled applicant, result in discrimination arising from disability, will be unlawful unless you can show they are a proportionate means of achieving a legitimate aim. (EHRC, 2015)

Therefore, any reasons for not accepting a learner onto a course need to be clearly justified in terms of them being unable to meet the aims of the course, even with *reasonable adjustments* in place. You need to ensure that you consult the learner, the awarding organisation guidelines and the relevant department in your organisation in order to find the best course of action for your learner.

Teachers are often under pressure by their employers to recruit enough learners to run a course, but potential learners should never be enrolled onto a course which does not meet their needs or abilities. Enrolling a learner without the requisite entry requirements is setting them up for failure. The short-term gain to your recruitment numbers could lead to poor retention, achievement and progression as well as disruptive behaviour stemming from demotivated learners.

However, adhering to guidance should never mean that we turn away learners from education. We must instead ensure that they are given clear guidance towards joining more suitable programmes. This could mean suggesting they enrol on a course that will gain them a qualification to meet the entry requirements later or that they consider available alternatives.

Question

What are the course entry requirements for your learners?

Aim 2: To identify any special education needs and necessary adjustments to teaching and assessment strategies

The Equality Act (2010) regulates that education providers are legally obliged to make reasonable adjustments to help learners with disabilities participate and achieve in education. Initial assessment is therefore an opportunity for learners to disclose any issues. It is crucial that your organisation has effective means of recording learner information such as special education needs and disabilities (SEND). Following the SEND Code of Practice 0–25 (DfE, 2014), this would inform a learner's Education, Health and Care needs assessment. Once information has been disclosed by the learner, the Act assumes that the organisation as a whole is aware.

Information about your learners' needs enables you to start planning any necessary adjustments to your teaching practice, assessment strategy and support arrangements. It is a good idea to compile the learner information into a group profile (see Chapter 7). This not only helps you to consider planning in terms of whole-group and individual needs, but also enables any other teacher of your class to quickly access relevant information about the learners. As learners change throughout their educational journey, you will need to regularly update this profile. For example, the adjustments that you need to make to your practice may change if learners disclose further information; sometimes a learner may not disclose their disability during initial assessment and recruitment, or issues could develop during the course. You will therefore need to provide opportunities throughout the course where they can further disclose any issues – for example, during tutorials.

 Case study 1

It's enrolment time on a hot August day. You are recruiting in a noisy, crowded room full of queuing learners waiting to enrol. You are under pressure to be as quick as possible *processing* the learners through the right forms.

Question

How do you think potential learners will view the organisation in the case study above?

Answer

Recruitment is often the first time learners see your organisation, so it should be an opportunity to show it at its best. Understaffing, disorganisation and queues will give your organisation a poor reputation and may lose learners even before they have enrolled.

Question

What impact is this environment likely to have for learners who may need to disclose relevant information?

Answer

A learner may be unwilling to disclose personal information in such an environment, meaning that your planning will be based on inaccurate information and may unknowingly exclude learners. This could lead to lower performance or even course withdrawal from learners whose needs are not being met. Remember that as a teacher you must give learners opportunities to discuss any special needs or other issues throughout the course – just once at enrolment is not enough.

 Case study 2

You cover a class for a colleague. A learner asks for handouts in large print as she has difficulty reading small print. You didn't know this and haven't prepared any.

Question

What steps are necessary to ensure that this issue does not arise in the future?

Answer

If the learner has told their course tutor about their disability then the course tutor should record and pass that information on to the learner's teachers. A learner is not expected to tell each teacher of any needs that they have, so individual ignorance of an issue is not an excuse. The responsibility is therefore on the organisation to maintain records which are easily accessible to all relevant personnel. When covering a class, always ask for the group profile beforehand to inform your preparation. This should be up to date and easily accessible (see Chapter 7). Clearly, to meet the needs of your learners you need to know what those needs are. Finally, remember that it is essential that information about learners is stored appropriately and securely in compliance with the 1998 Data Protection Act (see Chapter 2).

Aim 3: To inform learners of their current ability and development needs

Initial assessment results need to be given to your learners as soon as possible as they provide an overview of strengths and development priorities. Regardless of the subject qualification, initial assessment should include assessment of English and mathematics. English and mathematics are important for enabling learners to progress while enrolled on their chosen course and will be essential if they intend to progress on to higher level qualifications. Initial assessment may also encourage learners to address their needs through enrolment onto supplementary courses to develop these skills.

For initial assessment feedback to be effective, it should be given as soon as possible after the assessment. As with all assessment feedback, the results need to be explained to learners in language they understand, as well as giving opportunity for discussion about future development needs priorities and approaches to achievement.

Aim 4: To inform your planning in terms of the whole-group and individual needs of your learners

Initial assessment is essential for helping you plan your teaching and learning activities and resources. From the results you will be able to consider the overall ability of your group and adjust your scheme of work accordingly (see Chapter 7). As well as this, it should highlight which individuals may need extra support and how they can be best supported. Furthermore, initial assessment should show you which learners already have good experience and understanding of the subject and could be stretched and challenged further.

In this respect, it is surprising how many programmes work on a *roll on roll off* basis. This means a course where learners can join at any point of the year. While beneficial in the short term by boosting recruitment, it causes many problems in terms of organisation and pedagogy. By enrolling learners throughout the year, data systems must be instantly updated so that teachers know what adjustments need to be made to practice and have time to change their plans. As well as this, the support system must be able to operate quickly, so that new learners in need of support have access to it as soon as they enter the class. Finally, from a pedagogical point of view, it makes planning the development of your group's ability to take responsibility for their own learning very difficult; it is difficult to nurture a group working ethos in your class if it is constantly changing.

If you teach on a *roll on roll off* course you need to ensure that any new members of your group settle in as soon as possible and with minimum disruption to the learners who are already on the course. Disruption can cause learners to become disengaged and they may withdraw from the course. You may find that a one-to-one tutorial with the learner is useful in order to provide them with the necessary information about the course and to find out if they have any specific disability that requires adjustment to the learning environment or resources provided. You could help learners to integrate into the class quickly by ensuring that they participate in pair and group activities with different members of the class. You could also pair the new learner up with a responsible member of your class who could *show them the ropes* from a learner's perspective.

Case study 3

An initial assessment activity informs a teacher that the majority of new learners have extensive work experience in their subject, but three are new to the trade.

Question

In the case study above how might this information affect the teacher's planning?

Answer

You will need to differentiate the objectives, tasks and assessments that you prepare for this class so that all of the learners face challenging tasks as appropriate for their abilities. As well as this, set pair work and group learning tasks which encourage more experienced learners to support the less experienced learners. Other possible strategies are noted in Chapters 6 and 7.

SUMMARY OF INITIAL ASSESSMENT

Ideally, initial assessment should occur well before a learner is due to start their course. This enables the teacher to check that the learners are on the right courses, make sure appropriate support is in place and make necessary adjustments to resources and teaching and learning plans. If necessary, discuss the timing of any initial assessment process with your manager.

Learning-style assessments and inventories: the debate

During initial assessment, you may use *learning-style* assessments in order to identify specific ways in which learners learn. These results may be used to inform teachers' planning as well as learners of their best approach to study. However, Coffield et al. (2004) questioned the sufficiency of evidence to justify the validity and purported benefits of such assessments. Furthermore, the potential focus on the individual as a recipient of learning rather than as a contributor to group understanding and development undermines the power of education to be a fundamentally social activity. In terms of informing your planning, therefore, consider how information about your learners' learning styles could be used to help engage them as individuals and as a group into a discussion about how they learn – and how they can learn to learn better. Crucially, though, avoid labelling learners as having a particular style as this could limit their motivation and responsibility to develop a variety of skills and approaches to learning.

Whatever mode of initial assessment is used, it is important to engage your learners in a regular dialogue about how they learn and how they might develop their ability to learn. Doing this will inform you of what you can change to make their experience better, as well as what is often forgotten when gaining learner feedback: what *they* can develop in order to become better learners. Such a dialogue should be ongoing with your learners, both as individuals and as a group in order to develop learning skills, attitudes and aspirations.

IDENTIFYING LEARNERS' NEEDS AND GOALS

Let's return to your thoughts about your learners. Previously you considered the similarities and differences between your learners.

Question

What are your learners' needs?

Answer

You might want to consider this in terms of:

- o   qualifications;
- o   employment aspirations;
- o   academic/skills development;
- o   personal/social characteristics and attitudes.

Many courses are associated with a qualification which is part of the Qualifications and Credit Framework (QCF) or the National Qualifications Framework (NQF). Linking a qualification to the QCF or NQF has the benefit of providing the learner with a nationally recognised proof of achievement (Ofqual, 2015). The Introduction at the beginning of this book has provided some explanation of the QCF, as does Chapter 4. Successful achievement of these qualifications plays a part in the accountability process; it is one of the many ways that – fairly or unfairly – our performance as a teacher is judged.

SUMMARY

Identifying the learners' starting points, what they already know and what their specific needs are in relation to their learning can help you to plan and deliver lessons that engage and motivate all learners.

Check your understanding

You will find some suggested answers at the back of the book.

Activity 1: Read Scenario 1 and identify the potential impact of the comment made by the manager on: the learner, the teacher, the organisation, any significant others.

Scenario 1: A student wants to do a level 3 Teaching Assistant course. However, his initial assessment reveals that his level of English is Entry level 3 – which is below that required for the course. You ask your manager about alternative courses for the learner but she replies: "Oh, just let him on."

Activity 2: Read Scenario 2 and identify the potential impact of the comment made by the manager on: the learner, the teacher, the organisation, any significant others.

Scenario 2: You ask about initial assessment for a group of learners who want to enrol onto an IT course. The reply is "Oh, we don't do that. If they pay – they're on!"

Activity 3: Read Scenario 3 and identify the potential impact of the comment made by the manager on: the learner, the teacher, the organisation, any significant others.

Scenario 3: A colleague interrupts a lesson halfway through the course to introduce a new learner to the group.

Activity 4: How do you record learners' skills and qualifications and specific needs?

End of chapter reflections: Outline five key points that you have learned from reading this chapter.

 TAKING IT FURTHER

British Deaf Association: www.bda.org.uk/ [accessed January 2015].

British Dyslexia Association: www.bdadyslexia.org.uk/ [accessed January 2015].

BBC (2014) *The Educators* (podcasts): http://www.bbc.co.uk/programmes/ b04dwbkt [accessed Janaury 2015].

Coffield, F. (2009) *All You Ever Wanted to Know About Learning and Teaching but Were Too Cool to Ask*. London: LSN.

Machin, L., Hindmarch, D., Murray, S. and Richardson, T. (2015) *A Complete Guide to the Level 5 Diploma in Education and Training* Northwich: Critical Publishing.

National Autistic Society: www.autism.org.uk/ [accessed January 2015].

NIACE: www.niace.org.uk/ [accessed January 2015].

REFERENCES

Coffield, F. et al. (2004) *Should We Be Using Learning Styles? What Research Has to Say About Practice*. London: Learning and Skills Research Centre.

DfE (2014) *Special Education Needs Disability Code of Practice 0–25*. London: DfE www.gov.uk/government/publications/send-code-of-practice-0-to-25 [accessed January 2015].

EHRC (2015) *How Do I Avoid Discriminating Against Someone in Relation to Admission Terms?* www.equalityhumanrights.com/advice-and-guidance/further-and-higher-education-providers-guidance/admissions/you-must-not-place-terms-on-a-person-s-admission-to-your-institution-which-are-discriminatory/how-do-i-avoid-discriminating-in-relation-to-admission-terms/ [accessed September 2014].

ETF (2014) www.et-foundation.co.uk/ [accessed May 2015].

Ofqual (2015) *Compare Different Qualifications* Available from: https://www.gov.uk/what-different-qualification-levels-mean [accessed January 2015].

4 Assessment practices and processes

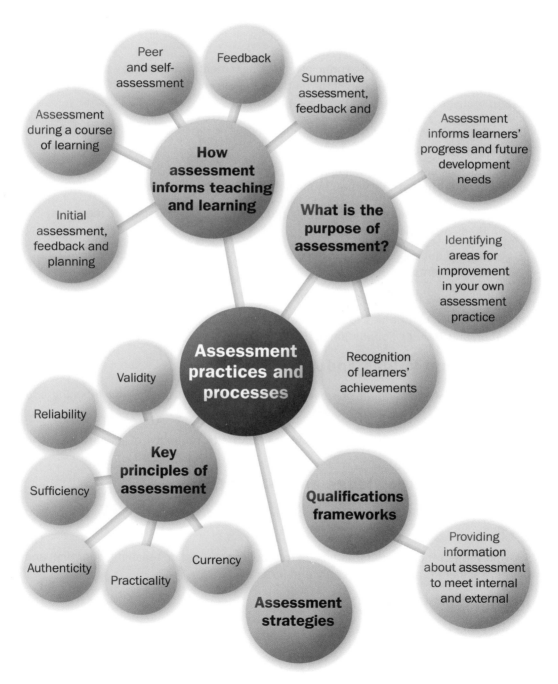

KEY WORDS

achievement, assessment cycle, authenticity, currency, equality, fairness, feedback, formative assessment, group assessment, individual assessment, peer assessment, practicality, reliability, sufficiency, summative assessment, validity.

PROFESSIONAL LINKS

This chapter focuses on the key principles of assessment, considering why and how we assess. Concepts about assessment run through many of the level 4 CET units but this chapter focuses particularly on the level 4 unit:

  o *Assessing learners in education and training (level 4): 1.1, 1.2, 1.3, 1.4, 1.5; 2.1, 2.1, 2.3, 2.4, 2.5; 3.1, 3.2; 4.1, 4.2.*

Throughout this chapter you will consider different purposes, types and approaches to assessment. In this way, this chapter aims meet the following objectives:

  o to develop understanding of types and methods of assessment to meet the needs of individual learners;

  o to carry out assessments in accordance with internal and external requirements;

  o to evaluate and identify improvements to your assessment practice.

This chapter also contributes to the following Professional Standards as provided by the Education and Training Foundation (ETF) (2014):

Professional Values and Attributes

Develop your own judgement of what works and does not work in your teaching and training

5   Value and promote social and cultural diversity, equality of opportunity and inclusion

Professional knowledge and understanding

Develop deep and critically informed knowledge and understanding in theory and practice

9   Apply theoretical understanding of effective practice in teaching, learning and assessment drawing on research and other evidence

Professional skills

Develop your expertise and skills to ensure the best outcomes for learners

13 Motivate and inspire learners to promote achievement and develop their skills to enable progression

17 Enable learners to share responsibility for their own learning and assessment, setting goals that stretch and challenge

18 Apply appropriate and fair methods of assessment and provide constructive and timely feedback to support progression and achievement

A list of all of the Standards can be found at the back of this book (Appendix 1).

STARTING POINT

What do you already know about assessment?

○ What do you think the term *assessment* means?

○ When was the last time you were assessed in relation to any job that you have held (eg test, assignment, appraisal)?

○ When was the last time you assessed someone else?

INTRODUCTION

You might not think it, but you are probably already an expert in assessment. As a learner, you will have been assessed many times. You may have taken examinations, written assignments or had observations to demonstrate your professional competence.

Reflecting on your experiences as a learner

Step 1: Draw a timeline, from your birth to now.

Step 2: Mark on this timeline when you have been formally assessed as a learner. It might look something like this:

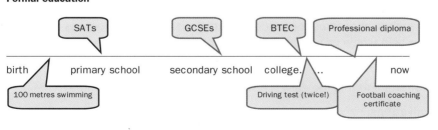

Step 3: Compare your timeline with a colleague and answer the following questions.

- How were you assessed?

- What was the value to you of these assessments?

Keep your timeline – we'll return to it later.

WHAT IS THE PURPOSE OF ASSESSMENT?

Assessment is an essential part of the learning process. Black et al. (2003) note that it serves several vital roles in an education system, such as:

- informing teacher and learner of progress and future development needs;

- recognition of achievement;

- providing accountability data on the performance of teachers, departments, education organisations and even international comparisons.

Black et al. (2003) stress the importance of conducting both assessment *for* learning and assessment *of* learning. Assessment *for* learning provides information to learners and teachers about the learners' current levels of ability. This information guides the teaching and learning strategies that are planned and prepared by the teacher. This is known as formative assessment. Assessment *of* learning provides information of learners' achievement and is usually summative rather than formative. Both methods have clear purposes and both recognise learners' achievement.

Assessment informs learners' progress and future development needs

Assessment does not have to involve taking an examination or completing a formal test. Assessment can be informal. For example, whenever you ask a learner a question, you are assessing. Any task you set them can be an assessment: How well did they do it? Do they need to go over this topic again? Each time you make a judgement of a learner's progress you are involved in the process of assessment.

Assessment informs the learner of their progress on your course and their future development needs. When supported by clear feedback about their work, they will also gain an understanding of how they can develop to prioritise and meet these future targets. For you, the teacher, assessment provides information about the progress of individuals and the group as a whole to inform your future planning. Following an assessment you might realise any of the following.

- Some learners find this too easy – how can I challenge them further?

- They're all struggling with this – should I revisit this topic?

○ A few learners don't understand this – what one-to-one/small-group learn
can I organise?

Question

Think of an assessment task (formal or informal) which you have recently given
to your learners.

○ What did the results tell you about their current and/or future needs?

○ If you repeated this assessment again, what would you change and why?

Recognition of learners' achievements

It is important to recognise that learners bring with them a range of differing experiences and qualifications in addition to those which were prerequisites for enrolling onto
a particular course. An initial assessment of each learner's ability prior to commencement of the course is therefore vital (see Chapter 3). Moreover, learners might be eligible for accreditation of prior learning (APL), which could mean that they would be able
to use credits from their previous learning to reduce the number of credits necessary for
any qualification linked to their current course.

Whether assessment is formal or informal, it can act as a powerful motivator for learners'
future development. For example, assessment of learning for a formal qualification opens
up career opportunities, such as enabling learners to practise a trade or gain promotion. Often learners' course progression options are only considered towards the end of a
course. However, to raise learners' motivation and aspirations and help them to develop
appropriate personal development plans, progression opportunities need to be discussed
and promoted throughout the course. Progression is discussed in detail in Chapter 9.

Question

Think about any of the qualifications that you have already achieved. How have
these changed your life?

Question

Following the completion of your CET qualification, what further academic and
career opportunities do you have?

Identifying areas for improvement in your own assessment practice

○   What qualifications are aligned to the subject that you teach?

○   Which assessment boards accredit the qualifications?

○   Taking account of the views of the learners, how effective are your assessment methods?

○   What are your organisation's requirements for internal and external verification of your learners' work?

○   How effective are these verification procedures?

If what you teach is not linked to a qualification:

○   investigate opportunities for formal recognition of achievement in your courses. For example, the National Institute of Adult Continuing Education (NIACE) have the Recognising and Recording Progress and Achievement (RARPA) scheme. This is: *a framework for ensuring that progress and achievement could be evidenced for learners and teachers in learning where there is no formal accreditation* (NIACE 2015).

QUALIFICATIONS FRAMEWORKS

Assessment can be an important part of promoting careers and employment opportunities through recognition of achievement for all learners. Nationally recognised qualifications are regulated by the Office of Qualifications and Examinations Regulation (Ofqual). These qualifications will be part of either the Qualifications and Credit Framework (QCF) or the National Qualifications Framework (NQF).

The Qualifications and Credit Framework (QCF)

Ofqual (2015) explain that the QCF qualifications follow set guidelines. They are unit based, with several units making a qualification. Each unit has a credit value, with one credit representing approximately ten hours of study. There are three types of qualification.

Award	1–12 credits
Certificate	13–36 credits
Diploma	37 + credits

As with the NQF, which we will cover next, each qualification is assessed at a certain level. This allows for qualifications in different subjects to be recognised as having the same academic value, as can be seen in Figure 4.1.

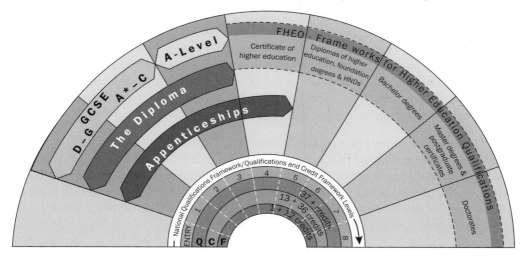

Figure 4.1 Comparing qualification levels (Ofqual, 2015)

The National Qualifications Framework (NQF)

Ofqual (2015) explain that the NQF is for qualifications that do not follow the QCF. However, they are still assessed within the entry level 1 to 8 framework, as illustrated in Figure 4.1 (an outline of the levels can be found in the Introduction to this book). If you are unsure about the levels of the qualifications you teach, find information about them on the Ofqual register of regulated qualifications or from your awarding organisation.

The UK qualification levels can be compared with other qualification levels in Europe through the European Qualifications Framework (EQF) (European Commission, 2015). Learners from outside the European Union can find out the value of their qualifications in relation to the English system through the National Recognition Information Centre (NARIC) (ECCTIS, 2015).

Providing information about assessment to meet internal and external requirements

As well as recognising achievement for learners, assessment is also seen as a means of evaluating the efficiency of how resources are being used in education. Assessment, in terms of measured outcomes, is integral to organisational quality assurance systems, and data about retention and achievement is used for accountability purposes. The UK education system receives a lot of funding from taxpayers, so it is considered important to be able to demonstrate that their money is being well spent.

In return for funding, teachers are expected to develop well-qualified and employable learners, and one means of measuring the effectiveness – or value for money – is through data analysis of results. This evaluation starts with your practice and organisation and may feed into national and international comparisons. One means of comparing education systems is the Programme for International Student Assessment (PISA, 2015, p1), who define their aims as: *to evaluate education systems worldwide every three years by assessing 15-year-olds' competencies in the key subjects – reading, mathematics and science.* In this respect, our educational achievement is largely assessed in terms of what is easiest to measure – through test results, which are then used to judge the effectiveness of the system as a whole, your organisation and your personal practice.

Nevertheless, this approach has been criticised. There has been an annual debate about whether examination results reflect improved teaching and learning or easier assessment, as well as whether they are fit for their intended purpose. Professor Alison Wolf's Review of Vocational Education (Wolf, 2011, p11) found that funding based on achievement of qualifications had led to a focus on quantity rather than quality, and Professors Frank Coffield and Bill Williamson highlight the potentially negative effects of constant testing on learners and their teachers (Coffield and Williamson, 2011, p46). Therefore, remember the value to learners of constructive assessment *for* learning as well as assessment *of* learning. This focus on constructive development as well as measurement of learning enables them to benefit from a balanced mix of formative and summative assessment. Finally, whatever assessment approaches are used, it is important that you maintain auditable information about your learners' progress for your institution's quality mechanisms.

Question

Consider the following:

o   How is assessment of your learners recorded?

o   How is learner achievement in your subject measured?

o   What are the perceived benefits of these approaches?

o   What are the main criticisms of these approaches?

Remember: always consider the impact on learners and teachers in your analysis. See the *Taking It Further* list at the end of the chapter for possible sources of information.

Question

Consider the following:

o   How does your organisation try to improve achievement?

o   To what extent is this approach successful?

○   How does your learners' retention and achievement data relate to the organisation/national benchmarks?

○   What are you doing to improve your achievement rates?

Assessment is a crucial component to learners' development. It is therefore important that you keep up to date with the latest developments in your subject area, in your organisation and in terms of national policy. You can do this through attending relevant assessment training sessions, reading current subject-specific literature and developing pedagogical approaches in relation to teaching, learning and assessment.

KEY PRINCIPLES OF ASSESSMENT

Now we've considered the purpose and value of assessment, it's time to think about key principles which inform effective assessment. Overall, the most important consideration should be that the assessment promotes equality of opportunity for all of your learners to succeed *to the best of their ability.* In this respect, learners need to feel that their assessment is 'fair' – that, as far as possible, the result represents an accurate picture of their ability in the subject.

Question

Using your timeline, reflect on your experiences of being assessed and consider the following.

○   Which assessments did you think gave a reasonable assessment of your abilities at the time? Which ones did not?

○   Did you feel that any of them were unfair on you or others? If so why?

○   Compile a list of what you think makes a fair assessment and what makes one unfair. Have you found any common themes? Keep this list so that you can relate your ideas to the key principles of assessment that we're now going to examine.

Figure 4.2 illustrates how key principles can contribute to the overall purpose of assessment, which is to provide equality of opportunity for your learners to demonstrate the extent of their ability and development.

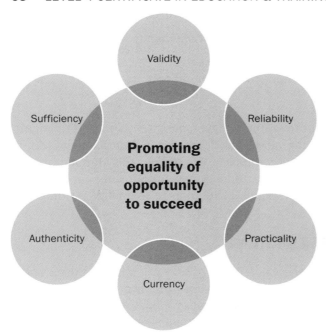

Figure 4.2 Promoting equality of opportunity through assessment

Validity

When considering the validity of an assessment, we are essentially ascertaining whether the means of testing is appropriate for evaluating the knowledge, skills and abilities required.

Question

A multiple-choice test might be reasonably effective as a means of testing knowledge. However, would a test on the *knowledge* of how to fly a plane be a valid assessment of a novice pilot's *ability* to actually fly one? What other assessment activities might you want the pilot to undertake before you got on the plane?

Answer

A test of knowledge would not assess the practical skills of the pilot – knowing how to do something is not the same as actually being able to do it. We would expect a pilot to also undergo a series of practical skills tests, for example, in a flight simulator, with a co-pilot and finally solo flying.

This might seem obvious, but actually you can question the validity of any assessment to some extent. For example, if you teach English for Speakers of Other Languages or a foreign language, you may give your learners a test of their listening ability. However, to assess this, their response will be either spoken, written or by reading and selecting an answer. So actually when you assess the skill of listening you are also assessing their ability in another skill.

Question

Return to the list of 'fair'/'unfair' assessments that you made earlier. Which of the issues you identified are related to their validity?

Reliability

Rust (2001, p2) notes that: *If a particular assessment were totally reliable, assessors acting independently using the same criteria and mark scheme would come to exactly the same judgement about a given piece of work.* Reliability can therefore be considered in terms of the extent to which:

○ markers assess work using standard criteria, interpreting these as objectively as possible;

○ different assessments for the same level and qualification are equitable in terms of the challenge they set for the learners;

○ the conditions under which an assessment is set are similar.

This means that all learners should undergo the assessment in conditions as similar as possible. In this respect, awarding bodies often give guidelines for the following.

○ The assessment criteria: what they are and how they should be interpreted. Assessors should 'standardise' marking prior to assessing a batch of work in order to check that they are interpreting standards/criteria in the same way. This is especially important in assessments where there is no clear 'right' or 'wrong' answer. Where professional judgements of competency are required, these may be interpreted differently, so require prior agreement to agree the appropriate standard.

○ Where an assessment is set: this might include instruction on how to set out a room so that all learners are assessed in a similar environment.

○ When an assessment is set: a national exam will often have a specific start time and date so that learners who have completed the assessment cannot communicate its content to other learners. Guidance will often include the duration of the assessment which must be adhered to in order to ensure that all learners are being fairly assessed.

○ Other course-specific guidance: this must be followed so that the assessment is fair for all learners taking it. This might include what equipment is permitted. A typical example would be mathematics, where some papers permit the use of calculators whereas others do not.

However, remember that promoting equality of opportunity does not necessarily mean *treating everyone the same*. Each awarding organisation has specific provision allowances made for learners with special education needs. You will need to find out what these are well in advance of the assessment so that all of your learners have the best chance to succeed. Typical examples of reasonable adjustments which an awarding organisation may recommend could include:

○   allowing a reader for some learners;

○   extra time allowances;

○   for language-listening-skills assessments, a specially recorded listening exam;

○   assessment papers with large print.

Question

An assessment asks for a presentation where learners have to *demonstrate good communication skills*. What issues might arise from having this assessment criteria?

Answer

Clearly, as an assessment criteria, it is too vague. Firstly, precisely which communication skills are we assessing? Secondly, what do we mean by 'good'? Good communication skills for an entry 1 learner would be different from those for a learner studying a higher education course at a college. Our expectations need to be defined and then their interpretations must be agreed by the assessors. This also demonstrates how important it is to make learners aware of assessment criteria. While these may be written in technical language unsuitable for their level of understanding, it is important that they are aware of what the expectations of the assessments are. This could involve demonstrating good examples of practice to the learners. Where appropriate, your learners could observe qualified professionals at work, see models of completed work or analyse examples of written work which meet the required standard.

Sufficiency

Sufficiency relates to the scope of the assessment. This means that an assessment should reflect a reasonable range of the topics covered (in the syllabus) as well as any skills and abilities developed. However, assessments rarely cover everything that has been taught, as they would become too long and impractical. Therefore a sufficient assessment is one that demonstrates coverage of key elements of the award syllabus and assessment criteria.

Question

An end-of-year French language reading examination consists of ten multiple-choice questions. Would this be sufficient?

Answer

Such an assessment would be insufficient. It could not hope to cover key topics in the syllabus or assess the desired language skills or to cover everything that had been learned. Also, with so few questions, learners could be lucky through guessing answers.

Authenticity

The authenticity of an assessment refers to ensuring that work submitted is that of the candidate. As an example, for examinations, most awarding bodies require that learners bring their identification cards which are checked by teachers.

Practicality

Generally speaking, the more reliable we attempt to make our assessments, such as through the use of varied assessment approaches and in-depth tasks, there is a danger that they will become impractical and costly to organise. This therefore means that there will never be a fully accurate and fair assessment – it will always be a balancing act between what is practical (and affordable) and giving learners a fair opportunity to demonstrate their abilities. We should also consider the impact that assessment preparation has on our ability to inspire and motivate our learners. While it is important that learners know and practise using the assessment techniques required in the final assessment, excessive preparation can be counterproductive. Learners may quickly tire of assessment-led learning where a teacher only focuses on assessment requirements to the detriment of instilling interest in the subject.

Currency

The final main concern of assessment relates to the value of the award – both in academic terms and with employers or professional bodies. This relates to the value of an award in relation to other qualifications and the extent to which it is up to date in terms of subject requirements. Does the award comply with the latest laws, policies and codes of practice of the relevant professional bodies and government agencies?

SESSMENT INFORMS TEACHING AND LEARNING

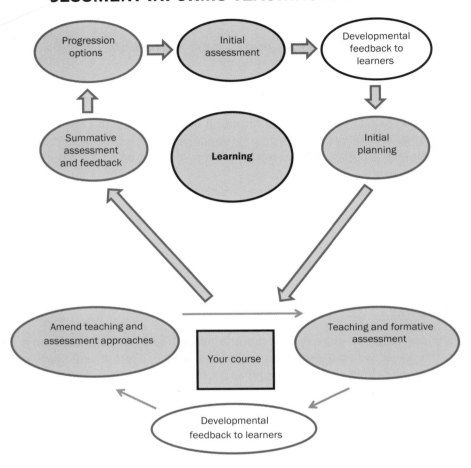

Figure 4.3 How assessment informs teaching and learning: an assessment cycle

Figure 4.3 aims to show how assessment should be an integral part of your course. This doesn't mean that you should be giving your learners examination practice all the time, but that you should be checking that they have grasped the key concepts, and are developing their ability to learn (and take responsibility for their learning) throughout the course. If we just assess at the end of the course, then essentially it's too late to remedy any problems the learners have had with your course or to change our teaching strategies to meet their needs. So a key concept to remember is that assessment isn't all about the learner. As well as informing the learners of how well they are doing, it also lets us know how effective our teaching is and what we need to change. If a student fails a course, have we also – to some extent – failed?

Initial assessment, feedback and planning

Initial assessment has four key aims:

○   to enrol a student onto the correct course;

○   to identify any special education needs and necessary adjustments to teaching and assessment strategies;

○   to inform learners of their current ability and development needs;

○   to inform your planning in terms of the group and individual ability of your learners.

For more detailed consideration of initial assessment, see Chapter 3.

Assessment during a course of learning

When learners are assessed during their course and the assessment is not part of the final grade, this is known as formative assessment. In contrast, assessments which contribute to the final grade are considered to be summative assessments. Summative assessments usually occur at the end of the course, but there may also be assessments throughout the course (for example, course work, presentations) that could be considered as being summative for each module or unit.

It is vital that you assess your learners throughout the course of their learning. This might be informally – through questions and answers (see Chapter 5) – or formally, through mock examination practice, for example.

Peer and self-assessment

Assessment should not just be teacher-led. Self-assessment encourages the learner to reflect on their own progress. When used in conjunction with assessment of your learners it can also show them how accurately they are able to judge their own abilities – encouraging them to take responsibility for their own learning.

Peer assessment is when learners judge each other's work. This has several advantages for learners. As with self-assessment, it encourages learners to take responsibility for their progress. Secondly, it helps learners to develop their understanding of the assessment criteria using active learning. This could be more effective than passively listening to a lecture by the teacher.

Challenges of peer and self-assessment

Nevertheless, peer and self-assessment can present problems for the teacher. As with any learning activity, careful planning is required in order to prepare learners for such tasks. Firstly, you will need to consider what they are capable of assessing. You need to determine which aspects of work they are currently able to assess and retain more complex elements for your expertise. An example of this could be a woodwork tutor getting learners to check that the correct measurements have been made by their peers, but initially retaining formative assessment of the quality of joints until the learners are capable of doing so for themselves.

Another issue relates to the language used to express assessment criteria. Awarding bodies often use complicated language to aid precise judgements, but it is unlikely that your learners will fully understand it. If you want to familiarise your learners with assessment rubric (the language of assessments), you must carefully explain key terms first. For example, terms such as *define, outline, illustrate, compare, analyse* and *evaluate* require increasing levels of contribution from the learner. Therefore, when engaging with peer or self-assessment, carefully adjust, limit or set the criteria by which you expect them to judge their own or each other's work – you cannot expect them to be fully qualified examiners in a subject they are still learning. Giving learners responsibility for assessment also requires them to develop maturity in terms of taking responsibility for learning and their attitude towards their peers. Insensitive feedback could be upsetting – even when accurate. Learners might lack the subtlety of language which teachers use to accurately yet sensitively and constructively outline weaknesses. Conversely, another problem of peer feedback is that your class may be reluctant to highlight legitimate criticisms of each other's work. Learners will then receive inaccurate feedback which could lead to a nasty shock when they receive their summative assessment feedback.

Therefore, peer and self-assessment have, like other types of assessment, advantages as well as disadvantages. Ultimately, however, they are powerful learning tools which will help your learners engage in the assessment process as well as develop responsibility for their learning and that of the group as a whole, as detailed by Petty (2009).

Question

Consider the following case studies. Identify the problems and outline how the teacher could overcome them to make peer and self-assessment an effective aspect of their teaching practice.

 Case study 1

Mutually shared ignorance

An ESOL teacher decides to let the learners peer-assess each other's written homework. He explains that he would like them to check each other's spelling and grammar carefully. The learners actively engage in this task and a vibrant atmosphere ensues with in-depth discussions about the texts taking place. However, while monitoring the class, he notices that not only do they sometimes fail to see inaccurate work, but worse, they are incorrectly changing work which was accurate in the first place.

Answer

The teacher has set the learners a task beyond their capabilities. If they could write accurately they wouldn't need to be in this class. Limit the criteria for peer assessment and make sure they are ones which they are capable of achieving. In this case, the peer assessment could have been limited to checking that their peers had included the content required by the writing test. This would only require them to use their general reading skills rather than specific grammatical knowledge.

 Case study 2

A mutual appreciation society

"I present you with a simple choice! Either die in the vacuum of space, or..." he *paused for melodramatic effect, "Tell me how good you thought my poem was..."* (Adams, 1986, p56)

A group of learners are asked to assess each other's micro-teaching lessons. Although these were well prepared and delivered, there were clear areas for development in each of them. However, the group only states the positives and ignores these flaws.

Answer

Actually, as an initial foray into peer assessment, such behaviour has the benefits of developing group support and highlighting positive aspects of learners' work. However, if this continues, the learners will not be gaining accurate feedback on the quality of their work. The teacher can set tasks to prompt more developmental feedback – for example, they could ask peers to identify three positives and one area for development, in order to foster more critical feedback.

Case study 3

The critic

A learner's presentation is difficult to hear as they are quiet and clearly nervous. During group feedback another learner states: *Well, that was a load of rubbish, wasn't it*? The presenter leaves the room in tears.

Answer

Engaging in peer assessment requires maturity not in age but attitude. Children can engage positively in constructive feedback just as adults can be petty, insensitive and offensive. As with the second case study, setting a task which emphasises identifying positives will be useful as a starting point for a new group to help build individual confidence and a social learning mentality. Tasks that encourage more objectively critical feedback can then be gradually introduced as the group develops, but even then, the focus should be on giving constructive feedback which identifies how improvements could be made.

Feedback

The value of any assessment is in the quality of feedback that you give your learners.

Case Study 4

How useful to the learner would the following written feedback be on a written assignment?

○   *8 out of 10 – well done!*

How useful to the learner would the following oral feedback be on a practical task?

○   *Well it's ok, but I'm glad you're not plastering my walls.*

Feedback can be more than just a judgement of ability but should inform future teaching and learning strategies. Firstly, it provides an accurate assessment of your learners' ability in your subject – an assessment *of* learning. This will show what they have achieved. As well as that, though, it should also provide them with developmental feedback that shows what they have not yet achieved *and how they can progress.* This means giving clear guidance as to how they can develop their understanding of the subject, as well as how they can approach future assessments. According to research by Black and Wiliam (1998, cited in Weeden et al., 2002), feedback is one of the most effective means of promoting learner achievement – but needs to be done using methods that are going to be most effective and helpful.

Feedback can be oral – such as during a tutorial discussion, written – for example, after submitting an assignment, or numerical – such as a percentage. Either way, it is essential that we pay just as careful attention to how we deliver our feedback as we do when planning our classes. If we've finished marking a large batch of scripts it's very easy to hand them out and then get on with the next subject. However, how much attention will your learners pay to your feedback? Will they just check to see if they've passed and then forget about it? Have you ever done this?

Feedback is such a powerful means of development that we must not ignore its potential to transform your learners' achievement. It therefore needs to be clear and jargon free – just as you check learning when you are teaching a new concept, you also need to check that they understand the feedback. Ask yourself the following questions.

○ How do your learners receive feedback on their work?

○ Does it say which parts of the assessment they did well or poorly?

○ Does it give clear objectives for future development?

○ Do you engage the class in activities to help them analyse their feedback?

○ How do you check that they understand your feedback?

○ To what extent do they plan their future learning based on this feedback?

○ What activities could you introduce to ensure that your learners reflect on their feedback and consider future improvements?

Summative assessment, feedback and progression

Summative assessment and any subsequent feedback informs the learner of their final achievement – whether they have passed and what grade. Nevertheless, as well as an overall grade, it is important that the learner has the opportunity to explore progression options – whether they have passed or failed. What are their career options or aspirations? What are their interests? This is your opportunity to encourage your learners in their present and future education. (Progression is discussed in Chapter 9.)

ASSESSMENT STRATEGIES

This section will now consider the tools we can use for assessment. All forms of assessment have advantages and disadvantages and different methods of assessment are preferred by different learners. Where possible, using a range of assessment strategies provides optimum opportunities to make accurate and fair assessments of learners' abilities (in a specific subject or topic). Remember that there are many different approaches to assessment, such as:

○ examination;

○ questioning;

○ case studies;

○ interview;

○ observed practical task;

○ portfolio of evidence;

○ written assignment or essay.

No one method is the right method all of the time, so, where possible, use a variety of methods.

SUMMARY

It is important to regularly assess what you students have learned; if they have met the learning outcomes and if they are ready to take any tests associated with their course. This chapter is intended to support your understanding in doing this.

 Check your understanding

You will find some suggested answers at the back of this book.

Activity 1: Remember the ten-question French test mentioned earlier in this chapter? In order to make this test more reliable, imagine we now change it to 1,000 multiple-choice questions, answered online. Why would we *never* do such a test?

Activity 2: Research the main approaches to measuring educational achievement:

○ within your organisation;

○ nationally;

○ internationally.

Activity 3: How does your organisation collect and collate key retention and achievement data?

Activity 4: Find out what provisions your awarding organisation as well as the organisation where you work have for supporting the assessment of learners with special education needs and disability (SEND).

Activity 5: If a learner was diagnosed with dyslexia what reasonable adjustments might be made during any formative or summative assessments?

Activity 6: Return to the timeline that you completed at the beginning of this chapter. Which of the qualifications you gained still have currency? Which would you need to renew in order to evidence competence in the area?

Activity 7: Think about the type of feedback that you give to your learners. How do you ensure that it is fair and useful?

Activity 8: Can you identify three changes to your practice which will make feedback more effective for your learners?

Activity 9: What is the difference between assessment of learning and assessment for learning?

Activity 10: How appropriate do you think the assessment tools and approaches that you use are in terms of gaining an accurate assessment of your learners' ability?

Activity 11: List the assessment methods and tools you use.

Activity 12: Choose an assessment strategy that you use and rate it in terms of the key principles mentioned earlier in this chapter, with 1 being outstanding and 4 inadequate.

- ○ Reliability:
- ○ Validity:
- ○ Practicality:
- ○ Currency:
- ○ Sufficiency:
- ○ Authenticity:

You should have given a score for each of the above. Now consider the following questions in relation to each one.

- ○ Why did you not score lower? In other words – to what extent is your assessment strategy successful?
- ○ Why did you not score higher? In other words, what are the flaws in your assessment strategy?

End of chapter reflections: Outline five key points that you have learned from reading this chapter.

TAKING IT FURTHER

In addition to the literature already commented upon in this chapter, you may find the following literature of interest.

Analysis: *Do Schools Make a Difference?* BBC Radio 4 Podcast: www.bbc.co.uk/programmes/b01b9hjs [accessed January 2015].

Gravells, A. (2011) *Principles and Practice of Assessment in the Lifelong Learning Sector* (2nd edn). Exeter: Learning Matters.

Machin, L., Hindmarch, D., Murray, S. and Richardson, T. (2015) *A Complete Guide to the Level 5 Diploma in Education and Training* Northwich: Critical Publishing.

Ofqual: Office of Qualifications and Examinations Regulation: *The Register* register. ofqual.gov.uk/ [accessed January 2015].

REFERENCES

Adams, D. (1986) *The Hitch Hiker's Guide to the Galaxy (a trilogy in four parts)* London: Heinemann.

Black, P., Harrison, C., Lee, C., Marshall, B., and William, D. (2003) *Assessment for Learning: Putting It into Practice*. Maidenhead: Oxford University Press.

Coffield, F., and Williamson, B. (2012) *From Exam Factories to Communities of Discovery*. London: Institute of Education.

ECCTIS (2015) *UK NARIC What We Do*, www.ecctis.co.uk/naric/What%20we%20do. aspx [accessed January 2015].

ETF (2014) www.et-foundation.co.uk/ [accessed May 2015].

The European Commission (2015) *Learning Opportunities and Qualifications in Europe*, http://ec.europa.eu/ploteus/search/site?f%5B0%5D=im_field_entity_type%3A97 [accessed January 2015].

NIACE (2015) *Recognising and Recording Progress and Achievement*, www.niace. org.uk/current-work/rarpa [accessed January 2015].

Ofqual (2015) *Compare Different Qualifications* https://www.gov.uk/what-different-qualification-levels-mean [accessed January 2015].

Petty, G. (2009) *Evidence Based Teaching* (2nd edn). Cheltenham: Nelson Thornes.

PISA (2015) *Measuring Student Success Around the World*, http://www.oecd.org/pisa/aboutpisa/ [accessed September 2015].

Rust, C. (2001) *Basic Assessment Issues and Terminology*. York: HEA.

Weeden, P., Winterm, J., and Broadfoot, P. (2002) *Assessment – What's In It for Schools?* London: Routledge.

Wolf, A. (2011) *Review of Vocational Education: The Wolf Report*. London: DfE, https://www.gov.uk/government/uploads/system/uploads/attachment_data/file/180504/DFE-00031-2011.pdf [accessed January 2015].

- Measuring readability
- Calculation of the Fog Index
- Jargon and specialist language
- Transactional analysis
- **Resources to enhance communication**
- Models and theories of communication
- Web-based resources
- **What is communication?**
- **Communication**
- One-to-one communication
- **Types of communication**
- **Communicating with learners and others**
- Non-verbal communication
- Listening blocks
- Communicating with large groups
- Communicating with small groups

KEY WORDS

communication, evaluation, Fog Index, jargon, noise, non-verbal, readability, receiver, resources, source, Transactional Analysis, verbal, visual, written.

PROFESSIONAL LINKS

This chapter considers the importance of effective communication within a learning environment. The concept and importance of communication runs throughout all of the level 4 CET units, in particular the following:

- ○ *Understanding roles, responsibilities and relationships in education and training (level 3): 2.2; 3.1;*

- ○ *Delivering education and training (level 4): 1.2; 2.1, 2.3; 3.1, 3.2; 5.1, 5.2;*

- ○ *Using resources for education and training (level 4): 1.1, 1.2, 1.3; 3.2.*

Specifically, this chapter also contributes to the following Professional Standards as provided by the ETF (2014).

Professional values and attributes

Develop your own judgement of what works and does not work in your teaching and training.

6   Build positive and collaborative relationships with colleagues and learners.

Professional Knowledge and Understanding

Develop deep and critically informed knowledge and understanding in theory and practice.

9   Apply theoretical understanding of effective practice in teaching, learning and assessment drawing on research and other evidence.

Professional Skills

Develop your expertise and skills to ensure the best outcomes for learners.

15 Promote the benefits of technology and support learners in its use.

18 Apply appropriate and fair methods of assessment and provide constructive and timely feedback to support progression and achievement.

A list of all of the Standards can be found at the back of this book (Appendix 1).

INTRODUCTION

This chapter provides consideration of key theories and methods of communication and asks questions and contains activities that are designed to develop your understanding of how to apply principles and theories of communication to your practice. In this way, this chapter aims to meet the following objectives:

○ to provide you with an explanation of some of the key principles, theories and methods of communication;

○ to support your exploration of ways in which you might develop communication with your learners and with others in your organisation;

○ to assist you in evaluating resources and suggest ways in which they can enhance communication.

STARTING POINT

What do you already know about communication?

○ What do you understand by the term communication?

○ What skills do you think you need to be an effective communicator?

○ How can the way that you communicate with learners influence their behaviour?

Effective communication is, without doubt, the most fundamental skill that any teacher needs to master. While you do, of course, need to be knowledgeable in your specialist area, you must also be able to convey that knowledge at a level and in a manner that your learners will understand. Your understanding and application of theories of communication will form a key part of your development as a teacher, as will your awareness of barriers that can hinder communication and exploration of opportunities to enhance communication with learners, colleagues and others.

WHAT IS COMMUNICATION?

An important starting point is to emphasise that communication is not a one-way transmission of information. Being a good talker does not mean that you are a good communicator. Perhaps you've experienced someone in your own life who is a great talker but has limited listening skills.

Models and theories of communication

Effective communication requires at least two active participants, one to convey and one to receive. This can be represented by a model of communication, for example, that developed by Shannon and Weaver (Hill et al., 2007). This model, while initially applied to technical communication, was also applied to human communication. At its simplest, this model can be considered to have two parts, a *source* and a *receiver* (Hargie, 2010). Therefore a conversation initiated by you as a teacher to a learner would have you as the source and the learner as the receiver.

The Shannon and Weaver (1949) model also recognises that interference, or *noise* can hinder communication (Hill et al., 2012). While you may instinctively think of noise in its literal form, perhaps people speaking, a telephone ringing, or noise from road works, it doesn't necessarily have to be. Noise can take a wide range of forms including visual distractions, disabilities or learning difficulties, languages or jargon.

Question

John is a new lecturer who needs to speak to one of his learners about their attendance. He teaches back-to-back lessons, therefore is unable to speak to the learner before the start or at the end of lessons. He decides to raise the issue while the class are working independently on a task he has set them. What problems can you foresee in terms of noise interfering with the communication?

Answer

You may have thought about whether a busy classroom was the most appropriate place to raise this issue. The physical background noise of the learners could be a problem. You might also have thought about the learner's attitude – would he be willing to listen to what you have to say in front of his peers or would he be too conscious of what they were thinking to focus on what you were saying?

Shannon and Weaver's model was developed by Berlo (1960), who further recognised that the transfer of information from the source to receiver was influenced by a range of factors (Hill et al., 2012). The factors that might influence communication at either the source or receiver include:

○ communication skills;

○ attitudes;

○ knowledge;

○ social system;

○ cultural factors.

Question

One of the influencing factors noted by Berlo is knowledge. If, as a teacher, you are the source and your learners are the receivers what influence would your knowledge have on the message that you are communicating?

Answer

Knowledge relates to the knowledge of the *subject* being communicated. Clearly, if you want effective communication to occur, you need to be able to talk confidently in relation to your subject area. If you have to refer to notes or keep pausing this will convey a lack of knowledge to your learners.

COMMUNICATING WITH LEARNERS AND OTHERS

In the previous example, you considered communication with a group of learners. However, for a large part of your teaching role you may find yourself communicating in differing ratios. You may be delivering a lesson to a large group, discussing a task with a small group, or communicating with individual learners. Each of these scenarios will require you to take a different approach and you may find that initially you feel more confident in one situation than another.

Communicating with large groups

New teachers often have concerns about large group communication. They realise that they are at the centre of attention and it can be a little nerve-racking at first. It may help if you remember that the vast majority of teachers felt the same way as you do at the start of their careers. Experience is ultimately the solution to overcoming these nerves, but you may find the 4 Rs strategy helpful in improving your communication with large groups.

○ **Relax:** If you are anxious you may find yourself rushing through what you have to say. Take your time and make sure that you are clear and confident in your delivery.

○ **Rehearse:** Don't be afraid to spend time rehearsing what you have to say in the privacy of the office or your own home. Effective teachers will always think ahead to what they are going to say. This is particularly important if you are teaching a new topic.

○ **Remember:** Remember that you are the one in the position of authority. You will know your subject very well. Remembering this and reminding yourself will help develop your confidence and resulting communication.

○ **Resources:** The use of effective resources, for example, presentation software, flip charts and whiteboards can help enhance communication. You could use bullet points on slides as prompts for what you want to discuss with your learners.

Communicating with small groups

You may find that you are teaching a small class of up to eight learners or need to split your larger class for group work. Either way, your strategy will probably differ from that used in large group communication. Your tone and volume will differ and you will also need to make efforts to ensure effective communication *between* the members of the group, especially if they are engaged in a group task.

One-to-one communication

Listening skills are an essential part of any communication process and are particularly relevant in one-to-one communication. Listening should not be confused with the passive act of hearing and requires active participation on behalf of the listener. It is therefore important when speaking to learners that you demonstrate active listening. This requires more than just paying attention to the words of the speaker; you need to consider your posture, your facial expression and, if appropriate, how you encourage them to continue what they have to say.

Active listening requires that you digest what the learner says and consider it before responding. Nodding, smiling or commenting at appropriate times helps to confirm to the speaker that you have heard what has been said. You also need to be aware of listening blocks which can affect you as the speaker or the listener and therefore hinder effective communication. McKay et al. (2009) describe 12 listening blocks and suggest that we may unintentionally use specific listening blocks with different groups of people.

Listening blocks

Table 5.1 *Listening blocks as noted by McKay et al. (2009)*

Block	Description
Comparing	Comparing yourself to the other person – are they smarter?
Mind reading	Trying to second guess what the other person is thinking
Rehearsing	Thinking about what you're going to say next
Filtering	Only listening to certain parts of what the other person is saying
Judging	Making an instant decision about the other person, accurate or not
Dreaming	Thinking about what to have for tea, your next lesson, etc.
Identifying	Linking what the other person says to your own experiences and telling them about it
Advising	Giving advice before you've heard what the other person has to say
Sparring	Quickly launching into disagreement with the other person
Being right	Never accepting that you are wrong
Derailing	Changing the subject to avoid a certain issue
Placating	Agreeing with what the other person is saying and avoiding confrontation

Question

Think back over the past few days when you have had a conversation with a friend, a learner or a colleague. Which of the above listening blocks do you think were applicable to your conversation?

Answer

Possible answers could include communication with colleagues as well as with your learners. In any teaching role you will need to communicate professionally and confidently with a range of other professionals, often adapting your approach accordingly.

TYPES OF COMMUNICATION

You can communicate with colleagues and learners in a number of different ways. You will use verbal communication, telephone and email, but you may also communicate via the use of images, letters or newer technologies, including social networking when used in a professional capacity.

The use of social networking is a growth area in education, with many organisations using blogs and social networking sites as a way of engaging with existing and potential learners; however, it is an area where you need to be particularly cautious, ensuring that you maintain your professionalism and be aware that what you share with others will become part of the public domain. You should only engage with learners in a professional capacity (for example, using an organisational social networking account) and *never* in a personal capacity.

Non-verbal communication

So far we have considered verbal and written communication and also communication using new and emerging technologies. However, there is one aspect of communication which is often considered even more important, that of non-verbal communication.

Albert Mehrabian (1981) considered communication and non-verbal communication in some detail and identified that communication was not just about the words used, but also included vocal aspects such as volume and tone and also facial expressions (McKay et al., 2009). In his experiments he found that when communicating certain words, vocal aspects were more important than the language used, and facial expressions were even more important. Non-verbal communication also considers body movements and gestures; our stance and posture and its importance as a key part of interpersonal communication should not be underestimated.

> ## Question
>
> A smile is an example of a facial expression that contributes to interpersonal communication. What others can you think of?
>
> ## Answer
>
> A frown, a puzzled look, a wink, a stare, a grimace, a smirk, a sneer, eyebrow movements or pursed lips are all facial expressions that contribute to interpersonal communication.

You need to be equally aware of how you use body movements and gestures. For example, if you stand in front of a class with crossed arms, you could be seen to be conveying a defensive attitude. Similarly, if you are holding a clipboard across your chest, you may be indicating nervousness. Consider the gesture that politicians frequently use when giving speeches; they use open palms to convey their honesty.

Of course, body language isn't an exact science. Your learners may be sitting in a cold class-room and have tightly crossed arms and hunched shoulders – in this situation the learner may be telling you more about the learning environment than how they are feeling!

One final word of caution in relation to body language: be careful to consider cultural differences before jumping to any conclusions. In some cultures, making eye contact with adults is disrespectful, certain innocent hand gestures have completely different meanings and handshakes can vary considerably, both in firmness, acceptability and duration.

RESOURCES TO ENHANCE COMMUNICATION

Resources are an excellent way to support variety, interactivity and communication in a learning environment, though you will probably find that the availability of resources can vary widely between organisations. Teachers in some organisations will have access to state-of-the-art technology including interactive whiteboards, video cameras and smart-phones, whereas others will have very limited access and may be teaching in remote locations, community centres and prisons, where access to some resources may be restricted. Wherever you teach, you should take time to find out what resources are available to you and how you can use these to enhance your communication and teaching.

The importance of resources is noted by Ofsted (2012, p48), who consider the effectiveness of resources, including *accommodation*, *technology* and *equipment*, as part of their inspection process. Often new teachers consider resources only in terms of books, handouts or equipment; however, they can take many forms, including:

○   stationery;

○   technology (eg educational and office software);

○   audio-visual (eg DVDs);

○   library / Learning Resource Centre (LRC) and written resources including books;

○   accommodation;

○   teacher-designed learning materials.

The final category in the list above is teacher-designed learning materials. These may be resources that you have created, or perhaps they have been created by a colleague and handed on to you. Whoever has created them, it is important that you continue to develop your reflective skills and evaluate these resources, both on their own merits and on their appropriateness for the groups you teach.

Question

Sam teaches Early Years courses at level 4. He has been asked to teach the level 2 course and notices that both courses have a module that requires him to teach a lesson on legislation. Can you suggest any problems that might arise if he uses the same handouts that he created for his level 4 course?

Answer

The key difference here is level. The language used in a handout designed for level 4 learners will probably be more complex and detailed than the handout for the level 2 group. If he uses the same resources without adapting them he could risk the learners not understanding the topic, being confused, or, at the extreme, starting to think they had chosen a course that was beyond their ability. (The Introduction gives further background to QCF levels.)

Measuring readability

You need to pay careful attention to the language used in resources, handouts, books and presentations. There are a number of systems available to you if you are struggling to decide on the appropriateness of a written text. One that you may find useful is the Fog Index, devised by Robert Gunning (1952). This is a calculation that, when applied to a text, gives a numerical value equivalent to the number of years of education a person would need in order to be able to understand that text.

Calculation of the Fog Index

1. From your chosen text, select a paragraph of around 100 words.

2. Divide the number of words in the chosen text by the number of sentences – this will give the average sentence length.

3. Count the numbers of words that have three or more syllables in your chosen 100 words.

4. Add the results from steps 2 and 3 together and multiply the total by 0.4.

Perhaps you could try this with one of the textbooks, resources or websites that you are thinking of using with your learners.

Jargon and specialist language

The Fog Index is based on the fact that a higher volume of words with three or more syllables can increase difficulty in reading. This seems a natural assumption; however, words of fewer syllables can also cause difficulty. Consider jargon, which is specialist language used in relation to a subject area. The use of jargon can often confuse learners or cause a barrier to effective communication. For this reason, you should be careful to consider what terminology you use and *always* explain any new words to your learners on their first use. You might also think about creating a glossary for your learners with words that they may be unfamiliar with. Leave space at the bottom to allow learners to add their own, and encourage them to review this at the end of each lesson, further developing their use of subject-specific language.

Question

What key words would be considered jargon within your subject area?

Answer

The list that you compile will be very different to that of a fellow teacher, though you may have considered acronyms that you use (words formed from the first letters of the words in a phrase) or key terms that you take for granted. For example, in initial teacher training we use terms such as inclusivity, differentiation and scheme of work.

Web-based resources

Many teachers now make extensive use of web-based resources and there is no doubt that there is a wide range of high-quality resources available to you to support you in your teaching, whether you teach yoga, sign language, functional skills, health and social care or one of over 200 subjects that are taught within FE.

Your choice of web-based resources does, though, require careful consideration. With many hundreds of millions of websites on the internet you need to be able to distinguish between the good, the bad and the ugly. It is particularly important that, in addition to evaluating your own practice, you evaluate the web-based resources that you use. You should be particularly aware that just because information is available on the internet, it doesn't necessarily mean that it is accurate, suitable or up to date. Always remember that anyone with access to a computer, the internet, some basic software and basic computer skills can create a website.

Table 5.2 will help you identify some of the things that you should consider when evaluating web-based resources.

Table 5.2 Evaluating web-based resources

Author	Who created the web page?
	Is the author knowledgeable/qualified in the subject area?
	Could the author be biased?
Purpose	Is it a personal or professional website?
	If created by an organisation, who are they?
Currency	When was the web page created?
	When was the web page last updated?
Spelling/grammar	Is grammar and punctuation correct on the web page?
Accessibility	Is it easily accessible and at the correct level for your learners?
	Is it suitable for any learners who may have a visual impairment?

Whether you use paper, electronic or web-based resources, they should also be evaluated to ensure that they incorporate equality and diversity, for example, in terms of gender, cultural diversity and disability. Your learners will all be different, with groups often comprising male and female learners from a range of cultures and with a variety of individual needs. These differences need to be reflected in any of the resources that you use.

Question

What changes could you make to your choice of paper, electronic or web-based resources to ensure that they incorporate equality and diversity?

Answer

You might have considered whether the images used in your resources represent different cultures, genders and backgrounds. You might also consider the names that you use in your resources and whether they similarly demonstrate diversity.

To ensure that your resources meet the needs of learners with learning difficulties or disabilities you might have considered the font size used, whether you were able to access audio versions for learners with visual impairments, or whether the use of coloured paper would be useful for learners with dyslexia.

TRANSACTIONAL ANALYSIS

The ability to analyse interpersonal communication is a key part of your ongoing reflection and evaluation of your practice. The theory of transactional analysis will help you to do this, enabling you to consider why some instances of communication are more effective than others and to start to analyse reasons for any communication breakdown.

Transactional analysis or TA is a theory proposed by Eric Berne (1964), which considers the way in which we interact with others. Berne suggests that we can adopt one of three ego states at different times.

Berne's ego states

Parent (P)   When we communicate as a parent – either controlling or nurturing.

Adult (A)   When we communicate as an adult – responsible, rational, logical.

Child (C)   When we communicate as a child – either free or adapted.

Berne's theory suggests that for effective communication to take place complementary transaction styles should be used. For example, if two adults are engaging in logical, rational and responsible communication this means that both of the adults are in an Adult to Adult state, talking and responding as an adult.

In another interaction, a hungry child may be asking a carer for food (they are using a Child to Parent transaction). If the carer responds as a parent and replies in a nurturing manner, they are responding as Parent to Child. This is a complementary transaction because the recipient is responding to the state in which they were addressed.

Question

If you address a learner using each of the following transactions, how would they need to respond to ensure a complementary transaction?

1. Parent to Child
2. Adult to Adult
3. Child to Child
4. Child to Parent

Answer

1. Child to Parent
2. Adult to Adult
3. Child to Child
4. Parent to Child

Whereas complementary transactions usually encourage effective communication, crossed transactions can sometimes lead to a breakdown in communication. Crossed transactions can occur when the other party replies in a different ego state from that in which they were addressed. For example, if a teacher asks a learner to work with another learner in class (Adult to Adult) and the learner refuses and says she doesn't want to (Child to Parent) a crossed transaction occurs.

There are occasions, however, when crossed transactions can be beneficial. For example, if a learner tells you they don't want to do their homework (Child to Parent) and you respond with: *Oh, I can see others have had problems with it, too. Why don't we have a chat about it later?* (Adult to Adult). Responding in an Adult to Adult state helps to calm a potentially problematic interaction.

SUMMARY

As a practitioner engaged in communication with learners, colleagues, managers and a range of internal and external contacts, it is essential that you are aware of how communication can be hindered or enhanced. You will need to be able to evaluate your own teaching in terms of a range of communication methods and resources, using relevant theory to inform your practice and making adaptations to meet individual needs. Ultimately, communication is the key to effective teaching, learning and professionalism within FE, and developing your skills and knowledge in this area will form an essential part of your professional development.

Check your understanding

You will find some suggested answers at the back of this book.

Activity 1: Write one sentence that defines communication.

Activity 2: What is the difference between Shannon and Weaver's and Berlo's models of communication?

Activity 3: Write down three examples of noise that can hinder communication.

Activity 4: Think back to a time when you feel that communication didn't go well. Your example may be in education, or it may be with a family member or even in a local shop.

You should reflect using the following headings:

- ○ What did each of you say?
- ○ What tone or pitch did each of you use?
- ○ What did your/their body language say?
- ○ What was your/their ego state at each stage of the dialogue?

Use your answers to the question above to suggest why the communication didn't go well and how things could have been done differently.

Activity 5: Evaluate one of your web-based resources using the following headings:

- ○ Who created it?
- ○ Is it a personal or professional website?
- ○ When was the page created?
- ○ Is grammar and punctuation correct?
- ○ Is it easily accessible and at the correct level for your learners?

Will you still use this resource following your evaluation?

Activity 6: Calculate the Fog Index of a written resource, book or handout that you use. Pick around 100 words and use the following calculation:

(average sentence length \+ number of words with three syllables or more) × 0.4

Will you still use this resource following your evaluation? If not, why not?

Activity 7: In terms of the theory of Transactional Analysis, what is the difference between complementary and crossed transactions?

Activity 8: Ask a peer to observe you and arrange to do the same for them, noting the extent to which non-verbal communication is used.

Activity 9: Consider the different communication situations in the table below and reflect on how confident you are in each, noting any evidence to support your evaluation.

Communication situations

	Large group	Small group	One-to-one	Evidence to support
Not very confident				
Fairly confident				
Confident				

Activity 10: Find out what resources are available to you in your organisation. You might want to consider them in the following categories:

- stationery;

- technology (eg educational and office software);

- audio-visual (eg DVD)s;

- library/LRC and written resources including books;

- accommodation;

- teacher-designed learning materials.

In what ways can you use these resources to effectively support teaching, learning and communication?

End of chapter reflections: Outline five key points that you have learned from reading this chapter.

TAKING IT FURTHER

In addition to the literature already commented upon in this chapter, you may find the following of interest.

Appleyard, N., and Appleyard, K. (2009) *The Minimum Core for Language and Literacy: Knowledge, Understanding and Personal Skills (Achieving QTLS Series)*. Exeter: Learning Matters.

Appleyard, N., and Appleyard, K. (2010) *Communicating with Learners in the Lifelong Learning Sector (Achieving QTLS Series)*. Exeter: Learning Matters.

Machin, L., Hindmarch, D., Richardson, T., Murray, S., (2014) *A Complete Guide to the Level 5 Diploma in Education and Training*, Northwich, Critical Publishing.

Mehrabian, A. (2007) *Nonverbal Communication*. New Jersey: Aldine Transaction.

Thompson, N. (2011) *Effective Communication: A Guide for the People Professions*, Hampshire: Palgrave Macmillan.

REFERENCES

Berne, E. (1964) *Games People Play: The Psychology of Human Relationships*. London: Penguin Books.

ETF (2014) www.et-foundation.co.uk/ [accessed May 2015].

Gunning, R. (1952) *The Technique of Clear Writing*. New York: McGraw-Hill Education.

Hargie, O. (2010) *Skilled Interpersonal Communication: Research, Theory and Practice* (5th edn). East Sussex: Routledge.

Hill, A., Watson, J. Rivers, D., and Joyce, M.D. (2007) *Key Themes in Interpersonal Communication*. Berkshire: McGraw-Hill Education.

McKay, M., Davis, M., and Fanning, M. (2009) *Messages: The Communication Skills Book*. Oakland, CA: New Harbinger Publications.

Ofsted (2012) *Handbook for the Inspection of Further Education and Skills*, www.ofsted.gov.uk/resources/handbook-for-inspection-of-further-education-and-skills-september-2012 [accessed July 2015]

6 Inclusive learning environments

KEY WORDS

behaviour, extrinsic, inclusive, intrinsic, motivation, policies, praise, procedures, reports, rewards, rules, safe.

PROFESSIONAL LINKS

This chapter considers what it means to provide an inclusive learning environment. The concept of providing an inclusive learning environment runs throughout all of the level 4 CET units, in particular the following:

○ *Understanding roles, responsibilities and relationships in education and training (level 3): 1.1, 1.2, 1.3; 2.1, 2.2;*

○ *Planning to meet the needs of learners in education and training (level 4): 1.1, 1.2; 2.3, 2.4; 4.1,4.2;*

○ *Delivering education and training (level 4): 1.1, 1.2, 1.3; 5.1, 5.2.*

Specifically this chapter also contributes to the following Professional Standards as provided by the ETF (2014).

Professional values and attributes

Develop your own judgement of what works and does not work in your teaching and training.

3   Inspire, motivate and raise aspirations of learners through your enthusiasm and knowledge.

5   Value and promote social and cultural diversity, equality of opportunity and inclusion.

6   Build positive and collaborative relationships with colleagues and learners.

Professional knowledge and understanding

Develop deep and critically informed knowledge and understanding in theory and practice.

9   Apply theoretical understanding of effective practice in teaching, learning and assessment drawing on research and other evidence.

11 Manage and promote positive learner behaviour.

Professional skills

Develop your expertise and skills to ensure the best outcomes for learners

14 Plan and deliver effective learning programmes for diverse groups or individuals in a safe and inclusive environment.

A list of all of the standards can be found at the back of this book (Appendix 1).

INTRODUCTION

This chapter provides information, asks questions and contains activities that are designed to develop your understanding and ability to apply principles of inclusivity to your practice. In this way, this chapter aims to meet the following objectives:

o   to provide you with an explanation of what constitutes an inclusive learning environment;

o   to provide you with an explanation of policies and reports that influence inclusive classroom practice;

o   to support you in providing a safe and inclusive environment for your learners;

o   to provide you with an explanation of types of motivation and ways to motivate learners in the classroom;

o   to support you in exploring ways to manage your learners' behaviour.

STARTING POINT

What do you already know about inclusive learning environments?

o   What do you understand by the term inclusive practice?

o   Why is inclusivity important?

o   What skills do you think you need in order to create a safe and inclusive learning environment?

INCLUSIVE LEARNING

An inclusive learning environment is one in which, as you would expect, every learner is included. If you cast your mind back a few generations, teachers used one approach to teach the whole class. There was no consideration of individual needs, and many learners fell by the wayside, having failed to match the way that they learn and their individuality to that of the teacher. Inclusivity requires that you, as a teacher, recognise that every learner is different and should be considered as an individual, with specific needs, likes, dislikes, background, motivators and behaviours.

In Chapter 4 you considered diversity, and knowing how your learners differ is the first step towards creating an inclusive learning environment. You need to make efforts to get to know your learners quickly and a range of techniques are available to assist you with this.

Question

Consider the example below and suggest ways in which Kuldip can find out more about the individual needs of his group of learners.

Kuldip has just got his first teaching post. He is teaching an *Introduction to DIY* class in an evening at a local college. He starts teaching in one week's time and has not been involved in the application process but wants to make sure that his planned lessons will meet the individual needs of his learners.

Answer

You might have suggested that Kuldip could start by looking at the learners' application forms. These should identify a range of information about the learners including:

o   age;

o   gender;

o   ethnic background;

o   qualifications;

o   disability or learning disability.

Having access to this information will enable him to start thinking about what individual needs the learners may have, though he should be careful not to make assumptions and should take time to speak to the learners individually as soon as possible.

Policies and reports on inclusive learning

Inclusivity and inclusive practice came to the fore following the 1996 Report of the Committee on Students with Learning Difficulties and/or Disabilities. This report, frequently referred to as the Tomlinson Report (1996), was a key contributor to the development of inclusive practice in FE. While its initial remit was to consider students with learning difficulties and/or disabilities, the outcome of the report noted that inclusive practice should be much broader. It made a huge leap and recognised that the approach taken to ensure inclusivity of learners with learning difficulties or disabilities was an approach that could be used to the benefit of all learners.

The Tomlinson Report (1996) emphasised that learners with learning disabilities or disabilities should be considered *first and foremost as learners* and suggested the *redesign [of] the very process of learning, assessment and organisation so as to fit the objectives and learning styles of the learners.* For you as a teacher, this focuses everything you do towards the learner and a learner-centred approach to teaching and learning. This also requires you to be aware of what motivates your learners in order to direct your teaching and learning strategies to meet their needs more effectively.

MOTIVATION

Motivation is what drives us to achieve goals. It can be affected by a range of different factors, among which are whether learners are intrinsically or extrinsically motivated. Some learners are intrinsically motivated. They are driven by a sense of satisfaction, by the pleasure of achieving something. They may have signed up for a course, engaged in an activity, or completed a task purely because of the pleasure that it gives them. Consider a learner who is attending a recreational art class purely for the joy of it. This learner is *intrinsically motivated*.

Intrinsic motivation is frequently considered in terms of the theory proposed by Abraham Maslow (1954). Maslow proposed that as humans we are driven by certain needs. A pyramid structure is frequently used to represent these needs, with the most basic being shown at the bottom. He suggested that basic needs must be met before learners can move on to higher levels and enhanced intrinsic motivation.

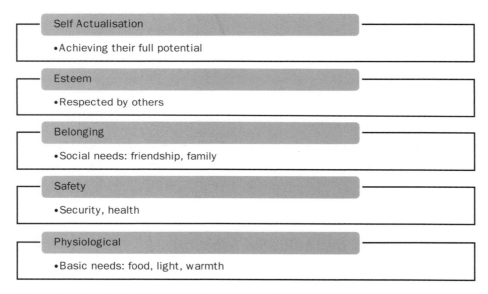

Figure 6.1 Maslow's hierarchy of human needs

In terms of applying Maslow's model to teaching, you should consider your learners' needs. Maslow (1954) suggests that we are all driven to move through the five stages to achieve our full potential, with the requirement that the needs of each stage are satisfied before the learner can progress. If you have learners who are hungry, it is unlikely they will be motivated as their basic needs are not being met. Similarly, if you are teaching in a cold dark classroom, this too will hinder learners' motivation.

Question

What could prevent *esteem needs* being met? How could you help to meet these needs?

Answer

For *esteem needs* we can consider a learner who has low self-worth. They may have been out of work for a number of years and feel that they don't have any skills to help them gain employment. To assist this learner, you could show them what skills they have and how these are valued by the group and society. If they are strong at a particular topic, you could encourage them to share their expertise.

Question

What could prevent *belonging needs* being met? How could you help to meet these needs?

Answer

For *belonging needs*, we can consider a learner who has just moved into the local area. Perhaps they have yet to make any friends and are struggling to mix with their peers in the classroom. To assist this learner, you could signpost them to the Students' Union social committee, vary the groups that you use within the classroom or even use a 'buddy' system, pairing learners up to work together through the course.

Intrinsically motivated learners are the type of learners that many new teachers expect to find in FE. Ask prospective teachers why they want to teach in this sector and many will give you the same response:

I want to teach adults – because at least they want to be there.

The reality is, however, often different. Not all learners are intrinsically motivated. Many are extrinsically motivated – they are driven by external factors, rewards, financial incentives or grades. Consider the learner who is attending a course because it will lead to promotion. This learner is extrinsically motivated.

Question

Consider the following examples and decide whether the learner is intrinsically or extrinsically motivated.

o John is attending an evening class in computing because he wants to get a job as a computer programmer.

o Baldish is taking a refresher mathematics class so that she can help her children with their homework.

o Sue regrets not taking GCSEs at school and has signed up for a pre-access course at her local community centre.

Answer

○ John is driven by an external factor – the new job. He is therefore extrinsically motivated.

○ Baldish is driven by an external factor – helping her children with their homework. She is therefore extrinsically motivated.

○ Sue is driven by a desire to better herself and is driven only by internal factors. She is therefore intrinsically motivated.

As teachers, you will often need to consider ways to motivate your learners. You may come across learners who are unco-operative, lethargic or lacking in interest. To ensure that these learners are included, you may want to consider ways of further motivating them, by considering the application of praise and reward.

Praise and reward

The origins of praise and reward lie with behavioural psychologists Edward Thorndike (1898) and Burrhus Skinner (1938). Behavioural psychology, or Behaviourism, is an early form of psychology which was based on the belief that behaviour could be studied through observation and without the need to consider cognitive processes.

Behaviourism was based on studies of animal behaviour, with Thorndike (1898) undertaking experiments in which a cat was placed in a box (which he referred to as a puzzle box) and needed to find a way out in order to get to the food that was placed outside of the box. The aim of this experiment was that the cat would find a lever that would allow it to escape the box and would gradually learn that pressing the lever resulted in it getting the food. Thorndike took his findings from these experiments and proposed that any behaviour (pressing the lever) that led to a favourable response (the food) would be repeated.

Skinner's work followed that of Thorndike and focused on a theory known as Operant Conditioning. In his experiments, a rat was placed in a box (a Skinner box). When the rat pressed a lever it was rewarded with food. The food became a positive reinforcement and led to strengthening of behaviour, with the rat learning that pressing the lever led to a reward. Skinner went on to suggest that strengthening of required behaviours could be achieved by the means of two concepts: positive reinforcement and negative reinforcement.

Reinforcement

○ Positive reinforcement is the positive effect of a behaviour. In the example above, the food was the positive reinforcement. This can be applied to a learning environment by praising a learner who answers a question correctly. The praise is the positive reinforcement.

○ Negative reinforcement is not punishment. It is the absence of any negative consequence. Consider the teacher who constantly grumbles when learners don't hand their work in. If learners hand their work in on time, the teacher doesn't grumble and therefore the negative consequences are avoided.

It is positive reinforcement that we will consider in this section. In particular, we will consider the use of praise. Praise is an excellent motivator and its effective use is a fundamental part of the effective teacher's toolkit.

Question

What are the benefits of effective use of praise in the classroom?

Answer

You may have included:

○ to motivate and engage reluctant learners;

○ to show learners that you value their input;

○ to ensure that learners feel included;

○ to create a positive learning environment.

Managing the frequency of praise is particularly important. You need to get the balance right and ensure that you use enough praise to keep learners motivated but take care not to give it unnecessarily. If you praise every learner every time they get something right, there will be little time left for any teaching and the praise will lose its value.

Praise can be delivered in a number of ways. It can be verbal, with comments such as *well done*, *good* or *excellent*. It can also be in writing on a feedback sheet to a learner (see Chapter 4). Praise can be just as effective using non-verbal communication, for example, as a smile, a nod or even a *thumbs-up* sign. The way you deliver praise and the phrases you use can differ according to your own style and the group of learners you teach, and it is important that you vary this based on the individual learner or learners in question.

Question

Consider two groups of learners. The first is a group of 16–18-year-olds studying functional skills and the second is a group of mature learners studying a recreational art class. How would your approach to praise differ for these two groups?

Answer

You may find that some of the 16–18-year-olds are lacking in motivation. They may have had issues with functional skills at school and don't want to be taking the subjects again at college. Given this, you would want to praise them early and often, helping to build their self-confidence. With the second group, as with the first, it would be helpful to know more about them as individuals, but as a teacher you should be careful not to assume that because the learners are mature, they won't need praise. Some of the group may not have attended a formal education setting for a number of years and may be equally lacking in self-confidence.

Rewards are a great way of providing positive reinforcement to learners. Don't panic, though, often the rewards that are the most effective are not monetary ones. You will be amazed at the excitement provided by a sticker, certificate or other non-monetary recognition of learner achievement. Some organisations have *Learner of the Month* and *Learner of the Year* awards, others do it on a departmental basis, and if you can persuade your organisation to find room in their budget for an annual trophy, this can go down particularly well.

If you do decide that you want to provide annual awards, you might want to think about how you could decide the recipient. Will it be judged or will you perhaps give out *golden tickets* at random moments? These can then be totalled at the end of the year and a trophy awarded to the learner with the most tickets. You might reward timely attendance, homework handed in on time or performance in class quizzes.

While praise is an excellent tool, it is something that should be applied to all. Sometimes teachers fall into the trap of using praise to motivate only the learners who they consider need it most. Be careful not to do this. If you are using praise, use it fairly, remembering to apply it evenly, as appropriate to the learners, but be careful not to overdo it. If praise and reward become the norm in your classroom, with learners being rewarded at every opportunity, you will have nothing left to offer when your learners need further motivation.

PROVIDING A SAFE LEARNING ENVIRONMENT

Providing a safe learning environment is at the heart of inclusive practice and is enshrined in the range of legislation discussed in Chapter 2. However, the practical application of this in the classroom requires that we consider wider areas, specifically the approach taken to manage behaviour. This is often one of the key concerns of new teachers in FE. You may have little experience in this area, other than recollections of flying board rubbers from your own school days. It goes without saying that we suggest a completely different approach.

Establishing rules

While a range of opinions exist in relation to managing behaviour, there are a number of common themes. Vizard (2007) suggests following the 10 Rs of behaviour management:

rules, rights, rapport, routines, relationships, responsibility, recognition, resilience, respect and rewards, whereas Cowley (2010) specifies her own fundamental rules of behaviour management.

Table 6.1 Rules of behaviour management (Cowley, 2010)

Rule	What it shows
Be definite	*I know what I want*
Be aware	*I know what will happen if I do/don't get what I want*
Be calm and consistent	*I'm always polite and fair to you*
Give them structure	*I know where we're going*
Be positive	*You're doing great*
Be interested	*You're people as well as learners*
Be flexible	*I know when to bend rather than to break*
Be persistent	*I refuse to give up*
Engage them	*I want you to learn*

The key to effective management of behaviour is to start at the beginning. Vizard (2007) specifically notes the importance of establishing rules with learners in the first lesson. Your learners may have come to you straight from compulsory education and may not know what to expect. At this point, you need to be careful not to impose a lengthy list of rules.

Question

What problems could result from a large list of imposed rules?

Answer

Firstly, if you provide too many rules, you are making things too complicated. Do you think you would be able to adhere to a long list of rules if you couldn't remember them? Also, too many rules may make the important ones seem worthless, so you should make efforts to choose only the ones most appropriate to your group of learners.

Secondly, learners may have come to you expecting a little more freedom than they had at school. If you welcome them with a long list of things that they can and can't do, it may well have the opposite of the desired effect, and a resentful group of learners will make for a difficult learning environment.

The key to effective classroom management is to get the learners to suggest the rules for you (with a little guidance and the odd nudge in the right direction, of course). This is the approach advocated by Marzano et al. (2003), who suggest involving learners in the rule-making process, though they do point out that some rules should *not* be negotiated with learners.

Question

What rules do you think should not be negotiated with learners?

Answer

Rules that cannot be negotiated with learners are rules that are laid down by legislation or organisational policy, for example. Health and Safety legislation or expectations laid down by an organisational behaviour policy.

Negotiating rules should be done from the outset. You might greet a new class with a cheery welcome and an introduction to the course before asking them to suggest what is acceptable in terms of the following:

o   mobile phones;

o   talking;

o   attendance;

o   mutual respect.

You must be assertive in this approach, though; you don't want the learners to agree to having their phones on for the entire lesson, chatting to their friends when they want to and coming to classes only when they feel like it.

By allowing learners to be central to the negotiation of the rules, you will often find that they start to manage the rules for you. For example, if at the beginning of the course learners have agreed to keep their mobile phones in their bags, and one of them subsequently takes their phone out, the rest of the group, who have been adhering to the rules, will quite often chastise the learner in question.

It is important, though, not to agree the rules and forget about them. Learners will need reminding about the rules as they progress through the course, and as they get more comfortable with each other (and with you as a teacher) they may be tempted to push the boundaries a little. For this reason, you should allocate time throughout the year to remind learners what they agreed to earlier in the year. Some teachers even get learners to create posters to display in the classroom, providing a visual reminder at every lesson.

Managing behaviour

While ground rules provide an excellent starting point for managing behaviour, you may still have concerns. You may have concerns about what kind of behaviour to expect in the classroom. Findings from Ofsted (2005) suggest that *the most common form of poor behaviour is persistent, low-level disruption of lessons that wears down staff and interrupts learning.* Ofsted (2005) further cite findings of the Elton Report (1989) to suggest that low-level disrupters can include the following:

○ talking out of turn;

○ avoiding work;

○ hindering the work of others;

○ being rowdy;

○ making inappropriate remarks.

The Elton Report *Discipline in Schools* (1989) promoted the need for a positive approach to classroom management in schools. However, its recommendations are equally applicable to FE. The report recognises the importance of appropriate sanctions, but emphasises the need for learners to be given responsibilities and to be involved in agreeing rules and behaviour policies. It further notes the importance of teaching and learning approaches and activities in promoting positive behaviour.

These approaches, where good behaviour is planned for, are much more effective than reactive ones (remember the flying board rubber?), which merely react to inappropriate behaviours and often have little impact on classroom behaviour overall.

Question

List ways in which you can ensure a positive approach to behaviour management.

Answer

The list is endless here, but you might have considered:

○ lots of different activities to interest the learners;

○ negotiation of rules;

○ creating and maintaining a positive and friendly learning environment;

○ making good eye contact;

○ reducing teacher talk;

○ effective use of praise;

○ effective use of reward systems.

Much of what constitutes a positive approach is considered as a natural part of what you as an effective teacher should do. For example, making your lessons lively and interesting and engaging all of the learners. You should also make efforts to quickly understand the needs of your learners, as individual behaviour issues frequently arise because of circumstances that teachers are not aware of.

Question

Consider the example below and suggest how James might respond to Jade's behaviour.

James is getting increasing frustrated with the behaviour of one of his learners. Jade is continually late for class. When she arrives, he challenges her in front of the group but she ignores him, puts her head down and takes her seat. She arrives late for the next lesson, ignores James, puts her head down and takes her seat, and so on ...

Answer

You should avoid making any assumptions or forming any opinions about Jade's behaviour without speaking to her on an individual basis. Before you consider any disciplinary procedures, you should take the time to find out the specific reason why she is late. Your organisation may have a discipline policy which requires that you issue learners with a warning for lateness, but before you take this route (which is reactive) you should speak to her to find out the reasons for her lateness. It may be that she has personal issues that are causing her lateness: she may be responsible for caring for her siblings, for example, and she may need to take them to school before she comes to your class, or she may have transport problems.

The physical learning environment

Creating an inclusive learning environment requires that you consider the physical classroom environment. You should consider where you will seat the learners and how you will ensure that they mix effectively with each other. You need to consider how you will avoid quieter learners being excluded and avoid the dominance of social cliques in the classroom.

You must make it clear to the learners that you are the manager of the learning environment, and you should do this as soon as possible. Cowley (2010) suggests that this should be done in the first lesson. Don't give the learners the chance to settle into their own groups. As soon as learners enter the classroom tell them where you want them to sit and make it clear that you will be mixing them throughout the course. They will join the class not knowing what to expect. But if you leave it until halfway through the term the learners will challenge your reasons for moving them and may even refuse to move.

Question

What other reasons can you think of for varying the seating arrangements?

Answer

You might have considered some of the following:

○   to encourage discussion and teamwork and develop their interpersonal skills;

○   to encourage peer learning – by varying the seating, learners will work with a wide range of peers rather than just their usual social group;

○   to accommodate different personalities – you might want to avoid having two strong personalities in the same group;

○   to provide stretch and challenge – you might put a more able learner with a less able one and encourage peer teaching.

LEGISLATION AND ORGANISATIONAL POLICIES

The co-operation and support of your organisation is essential in ensuring and maintaining effective classroom and behaviour management, therefore it is important that you spend some time finding out what policies and procedures exist to support you.

Most organisations have a behaviour policy with the aim of providing a safe environment for their staff and learners. These behaviour policies will be informed by a range of legislation (see Chapter 2), including:

○   The Equality Act (2010);

○   The Children Act (2004);

○   The Human Rights Act (1998);

○   The Health and Safety at Work Act (1974).

The policy should include guidance and expectations in a number of key areas, including the following.

○   Student expectations

  –   This should make it clear what the organisation expects of the learners in terms of behaviour.

○   Staff expectations

  –   This should clearly state what the organisation expects of the staff in terms of their behaviour and how they respond to learners' behaviour.

○   Disciplinary procedures

  –   The disciplinary procedure may be included as part of the policy or it may be a standalone procedure, and it should make it clear what will happen if learners do not adhere to rules.

  –   Disciplinary procedures usually follow three stages, with the first being an informal discussion, followed by a formal warning, and ultimately exclusion.

○ Rewards

– In addition to disciplinary procedures, it is important that an organisational behaviour policy considers how good behaviour will be encouraged. While you can put your own reward systems in place, these need to be applied consistently to ensure effective behaviour management across the organisation.

SUMMARY

Inclusivity is at the heart of everything you do as a teacher. You need to consider not only the individual differences between learners but also what motivates them and how you will capture this information to inform your teaching. You will also need to consider what strategies you will use to create a positive learning environment and make time to find out about your learners in order to build the professional relationships that are essential within any learning environment.

 Check your understanding

You will find some suggested answers at the back of this book.

Activity 1: Write one sentence that defines an inclusive learning environment.

Activity 2: Why do you need to get to know your learners quickly?

Activity 3: Write in one sentence the difference between positive and negative reinforcement.

Activity 4: Suggest at least three positive reinforcers that you can use in the classroom.

Activity 5: Why is it important that rules are established as soon as possible?

Activity 6: Why should you make efforts to negotiate rather than impose classroom rules?

Activity 7: What is the difference between intrinsic and extrinsic motivation? Which is easier as a teacher to provide?

Activity 8: What is the name of the key government report that contributed to the focus on inclusivity within the FE sector? What did this report say could benefit all learners?

Activity 9: Consider a group of learners that you teach. What rules might be appropriate for this group of learners? Why might rules differ between different groups?

Activity 10: Find out what policies and procedures exist in your organisation for managing behaviour.

End of chapter reflections: Outline five key points that you have learned from reading this chapter.

 TAKING IT FURTHER

In addition to the literature already commented upon in this chapter you may find the following literature of interest.

Machin, L., Hindmarch, D., Richardson, T., Murray, S., (2014) A Complete Guide to the Level 5 Diploma in Education and Training, Northwich, Critical Publishing.

Smith, J., and Spurling, A. (2002) *Understanding Motivation for Lifelong Learning*. Exeter: National Institute of Adult Continuing Education.

Tummons, J., and Powell, S. (2011) *Inclusive Practice in the Lifelong Learning Sector* (Achieving QTLS Series). Exeter: Learning Matters.

Wallace, S. (2007) *Managing Behaviour in the Lifelong Learning Sector* (Achieving QTLS Series). Exeter, Learning Matters.

Woollard, J., (2010) *Psychology for the Classroom: Behaviourism*. Oxon: Routledge.

REFERENCES

Benson, N., Collin, C., Ginnsburg, J., Grand, V., Lazyan, M., Weeks, M. (2012) *The Psychology Book*. London: Dorling Kindersley.

Cowley, S. (2010) *Getting the Buggers to Behave* (4th edn). London: Continuum.

Elton, R. (1989) *Discipline in Schools. Report of the Committee of Inquiry Chaired by Lord Elton*. London: HMSO.

ETF (2014) www.et-foundation.co.uk/ [accessed May 2015].

Maslow, A. H. (1954) *Motivation and Personality*. New York: Harper and Row.

Marzano R.J., Marzano, J.S. & Pickering, D.J. (2003) *Classroom Management That Works: Research-Based Strategies for Every Teacher*, ASCD, VA.

Ofsted (2005) *Managing Challenging Behaviour*. London: HMSO.

Tomlinson, J. (1996) *Inclusive Learning: Principles and Recommendations, a Summary of the Findings of the Learning Difficulties and/or Disabilities Committee*. London: HMSO.

Vizard, D. (2007) *How To Manage Behaviour in Further Education*. London: Paul Chapman Publishing.

KEY WORDS

affective domain, aims, cognitive domain, differentiation, functional skills, Minimum Core, objectives, planning, psychomotor domain, SMART objectives, wider skills.

PROFESSIONAL LINKS

This chapter considers planning and delivery in the FE sector. The idea of planning and delivery runs throughout all of the level 4 CET units, in particular the following units:

- ○ *Planning to meet the needs of learners in education and training (level 4): 2.1, 2.2, 2.3, 2.4; 3.1, 3.2; 4.2;*

- ○ *Delivering education and training (level 4): 4.1, 4.2; 5.2.*

Specifically, it also contributes to the following Professional Standards as provided by the ETF (2014).

Professional skills

Develop your expertise and skills to ensure the best outcomes for learners

13 Motivate and inspire learners to promote achievement and develop their skills to enable progression.

14 Plan and deliver effective learning programmes for diverse groups or individuals in a safe and inclusive environment.

16 Address the mathematics and English needs of learners and work creatively to overcome individual barriers to learning.

A list of all of the Standards can be found at the back of this book (Appendix 1).

INTRODUCTION

This chapter provides information about the planning and delivery of teaching and learning. It also asks questions and contains activities that are designed to develop your understanding and skills in planning and delivering effective lessons. In this way, this chapter aims to meet the following objectives:

- ○ to provide you with an explanation of what constitutes effective planning in FE;

- ○ to support you in writing aims and objectives;

- ○ to provide you with an explanation of the different learning domains you should consider when planning for your learners;

- ○ to support you in planning to meet learners' needs in relation to functional and wider skills;

- ○ to support you in applying knowledge and understanding of the Minimum Core to your lesson planning and delivery.

STARTING POINT

What do you already know about planning and delivery?

o Why is planning important?

o What documents do you need to complete to evidence your planning?

o What skills and knowledge do you think you need in order to plan an effective lesson?

o What should a teaching and learning plan contain?

For every subject area in FE, courses and lessons must have a clear structure and this doesn't happen by chance. Before you even consider setting foot inside the classroom, you need to focus on:

o course and lesson planning;

o making it clear what you want your learners to learn and when you want them to learn it;

o what activities and resources you will use;

o how you will assess your learners and how their individual needs will be met.

LEARNER-CENTRED PLANNING

Individual learner needs

Chapters 3 and 6 have emphasised the need to plan to meet individual learners' needs and suggested ways in which this could be achieved. This is something that should happen at the planning stage, with learners' needs informing the way that you plan your lessons and given important consideration from the outset. You may find that you need to adapt a lesson to suit learners with specific disabilities. Doing this doesn't necessarily only involve consideration of the content. You will need to consider how you use a wide range of resources, including the classroom or learning environment itself as well as any resources that you, or others, prepare.

Question

You have been advised that one of your new learners is a wheelchair user. What adaptations might you need to make in order to ensure equality for this learner?

Answer

Ideally, you would be given the opportunity to speak to the learner to find out their specific requirements, but you might have considered some of the following:

- Arrange for an adjustable-height desk which will give the extra clearance that may be necessary to accommodate the wheelchair.

- Review the layout of tables in your classroom. Is the whole of the classroom accessible to the learner? How can it be improved?

- Evacuation procedures – if you gain access to a classroom via a lift, you will need to find out what the evacuation procedures are for your learner in case of a fire or emergency.

- Are you planning to use any outdoor spaces or external visits? Will any adjustments need to be made?

In addition to planning to meet the needs of learners with disabilities, you will need to incorporate the suggestions from Chapters 3 and 6 at the planning stage in order to meet the needs of all learners. Your organisation will usually expect you to document how you will do this. You may note some of the following on the teaching and learning plan:

- handouts are provided on coloured paper;

- coloured overlays are provided for learners with dyslexia;

- large-print handouts are provided for learners with visual impairments;

- all resources and topics consider equality and diversity throughout.

Question

What other individual needs may you need to consider at the planning stage of your lesson?

Answer

You might have considered learning disabilities, race, gender, age, background, culture, prior experience and learning styles.

Group profiles

Being aware of your learners' individual needs is the first step in supporting them, but your organisation will usually require you to create a written record of what these needs are and what you will do to ensure that they are met.

Your organisation will usually provide you with guidance about what to include in a group profile; however, you may wish to include some of the following:

- age;

- prior experience;

○   any disabilities and/or learning disabilities and what support will be offered;

○   any attendance issues and how you overcome them;

○   any behaviour issues and strategies you use to avoid these;

○   preferred learning style;

○   target and stretch grades (this evidences good consideration of differentiation and encouraging the learner to achieve their full potential);

○   any friendship groups or conflicts with other learners and how you plan to ensure these don't hinder learning.

Question

What else might you want to document in your group profile?

Answer

You might have considered some of the following:

○   initial assessment results in mathematics or English;

○   entry qualifications;

○   assignment grades;

○   any personal issues that you are aware of and what support is provided (perhaps by a personal tutor or counsellor).

MEETING CURRICULUM REQUIREMENTS

For many teachers in FE, planning of a course and lessons will be informed by awarding body or organisational requirements. If this is the case, you will have set topics and often pre-set learning outcomes that must be met in order that learners can meet the required standards and have the required skills and knowledge to pass any assessment.

When considering curriculum requirements you will also need to consider the level of the subject matter. You may be teaching the same topics but at a range of different levels. We can take health and safety as an example: at level 1 you will probably be teaching basic subject facts and skills, whereas at level 3 you may be asked to teach in more depth about responsibilities, procedures and generally examine the subject in greater detail and expect higher level work from your learners.

PLANNING DOCUMENTATION

Your organisation will expect you to document your planning in a number of ways, evidencing both short- and long-term planning in order to meet individual learners' needs. You will therefore also need to know how to prepare and to have available a number of different documents.

Schemes of work

A scheme of work is a document used to evidence long-term planning. It is created before the course starts and spans the duration of the course, specifying the content for each week. The amount of detail required on a scheme of work can vary between organisations; however, at a minimum it should specify what you want your learners to learn (the learning objectives), your teaching methods, assessment methods (formative and summative) and resources.

The scheme of work helps you to structure your planning, allowing you to see the course at a glance. It will help you to ensure a logical order and that you allocate the appropriate amount of time for each topic.

Question

What are the advantages of using a scheme of work over planning a course week by week?

Answer

Using a scheme of work will enable you to see exactly where each lesson lies within the course – you will be able to ensure that you have enough time allocated to each topic and to group similar themes.

Most organisations will have a template that you should use for your scheme of work (an example template can be found in Appendix 2), though most schemes of work contain the same types of information, which will probably include the following.

○ **Timing:** This will include the length of the lesson (in minutes/hours) and the length of the course (in weeks or number of lessons). You will also need to take into account breaks, which may take place part-way through your lesson.

○ **Content:** You will need to state what you want the learners to learn. This will often be in the form of objectives or learning outcomes, though some organisations may ask you to list weekly topics instead. (Objectives are considered further as part of the discussion on teaching and learning plans.)

○ **Methods:** You will need to be clear about what teaching and learning activities you will use. Perhaps you plan to use games, quizzes, lecture elements, video clips, group work, discussions, etc. You should document all of these on your scheme of work.

○ **Resources:** Having decided what you're going to teach, you need to consider what resources you will need access to. You may need to create the resources yourself – for example, handouts, games and flashcards; however, you will also need to think about what other resources you will need, for example, computers, rooming or subject-specific resources.

○ **Assessment:** You will need to document the methods you will be using to assess the learners. This should include both formative and summative assessment and demonstrate that you use a range of assessment methods throughout your course.

It is important to note at this point that a scheme of work should be flexible. An effective teacher will not hesitate to change their scheme of work if they feel it is necessary. You may find that you initially allocated a week to teach your learners a particular topic and they are struggling to grasp the concepts. If this is the case, you might want review your scheme of work, adapting the content in order to give the learners an extra week to consolidate their learning and ensure effective progress. You might also find it useful to make notes on your scheme of work, noting what worked and what didn't and what adaptations you would make when teaching the course again.

Teaching and learning plans

Once you have completed your scheme of work you have laid the foundations for your planning; the next step is to consider your teaching and learning plans. While you have provided a brief overview of each lesson on your scheme of work, you will now need to expand on this and provide the details for your plans. If you have only provided topics on your scheme of work, you will need to provide objectives. A template for a teaching and learning plan can be found in Appendix 4.

Aims and objectives

Any discussion about aims and objectives needs to start with the difference between the two. An aim is a statement about what is to be achieved overall, whereas objectives are the steps needed to achieve an aim. Consider the following example:

○ *Aim: To improve learners' functional skills in English*

This is a broad statement of what you want to achieve, and while it does give some specifics – for example, 'functional skills' and 'English' – there is no detail about how the aim will be achieved. What the aim doesn't tell us is exactly what the learners will learn. For example, will they focus on speaking and listening, writing or reading? To what extent will they focus on each?

When you are planning any lesson, you need to make decisions about what you will teach and, more specifically, what you want the learners to be able to do at the end of the lesson that they couldn't do at the beginning. This is the role of objectives (or learning outcomes).

Objectives are statements that include an active verb. For example:

○ *Write* a story

○ *Read* a book

○ *Recite* a poem

The detail on the objectives above is limited and needs further work. This is where the SMART acronym can help. When you write objectives, you should ensure that they are specific, measurable, achievable, relevant and time bound.

SMART objectives

Specific: The objective should have enough detail to show exactly what learners are to learn. It must contain an active verb and shouldn't include words like *know* or *understand*.

Measurable: You should be able to use an appropriate assessment method to ensure that learning has taken place.

Achievable: The objective should challenge the learners, while not being set too high that learners will have little chance of achieving it.

Relevant: All objectives should be relevant to the course or lesson in question. As a teacher, it is your responsibility to plan to ensure that all activities and objectives fit with what the learners need to learn.

Time bound: When writing an objective you should be clear on the timescale in which it can be achieved. Many teaching and learning plans precede objectives with the following statement: *By the end of the lesson, learners will be able to* – this helps to ensure that the objective is time bound (it restricts achievement of the objective to the specific lesson).

Question

On an A level History course, learners are set the following objective:

Understand about the First World War.

Can you see any problem with this objective?

Answer

The problem with the above objective is that it is too broad and not specific. The First World War is a huge topic, so this needs to be broken down further. Perhaps a more appropriate objective would be:

State the sequence of events that led to the start of the First World War.

In this example, *state* is the active verb that replaces *understand*, and more detail has been added about what the learners should be able to do at the end of the lesson that they couldn't do at the beginning.

You should now be more aware of what is required in an effective written objective. It should be SMART and needs to include an active verb, avoiding any more general terms, for example, *know, understand* or *comprehend*.

Differentiating objectives

You will be expected to write objectives for every teaching and learning plan and your organisation will probably expect you to differentiate these. This means that while you expect a certain achievement from all of your learners, you will need to have higher expectations of the more able learners and provide *all* learners with stretch and challenge. On a teaching and learning plan you may be asked to write objectives under the following headings:

○   *all learners must...* (this is what you expect everyone to achieve but should provide stretch and challenge);

○   *some learners will...* (the objectives under this heading will start to stretch the learners further);

○   *a few learners may...* (the objectives under these headings will provide the greatest stretch and challenge).

Learning domains

Your choice of verb will be influenced by whether you are teaching knowledge, skills or attitudes. These are often referred to in terms of learning domains and it should help you to be more aware of your own teaching practice by considering these further.

The cognitive domain

The concept of the cognitive domain was developed by Benjamin Bloom (Bloom et al., 1956) and relates to the teaching of knowledge or thinking skills, for example, remembering a poem, comparing two different viewpoints or proposing a theory. Bloom suggested several levels with increasing complexity, ranging from basic recall of facts at the lowest level to evaluation at the highest.

If your teaching relates mainly to the cognitive domain, teaching methods you could use include lecture, question and answer (Q&A), gapped handout, card-matching activities or quizzes.

Question

What kinds of subjects could be considered within the cognitive domain?

Answer

While all subjects contain some element of knowledge and therefore will be considered as part of the cognitive domain, subjects such as law, sociology, psychology or history are all heavily dependent on knowledge.

The psychomotor domain

The concept of the psychomotor domain is attributed to Simpson (1966) or to Dave (1970) and relates to the teaching of physical or practical skills, for example, catching a ball, building a wall or riding a bike. The psychomotor domain has similar levels of complexity to the cognitive domain, ranging from imitation at the lowest level (copying the movements of someone else) to naturalisation. This higher level can be considered in terms of someone performing a task without having to think about it. Think about when you learned to ride a bike or drive a car. When you started out, you had to focus on what you needed to do with your arms or legs and what movements you had to make. After a little while, though, when you had mastered the skills, you will have found yourself making the required movements without giving it a second thought. This is naturalisation.

If your teaching relates to the psychomotor domain, your teaching methods could include demonstration, simulation and corrected practice – in corrected practice, you encourage the learner to practise the skill they have learned, with your role being that of a facilitator, stepping in to support the learner if they need further guidance and to ensure they master the skill correctly.

Question

What kinds of subjects could be considered within the psychomotor domain?

Answer

You might have considered practical subjects including vocational engineering, construction, sport and dance. All of these will have a large element of teaching in the psychomotor domain. Of course, underpinning these practical psychomotor skills will be a range of knowledge in the cognitive domain. Consider construction – being able to build a wall certainly requires psychomotor skills, but learners also need to have wider knowledge, for example, knowledge about brick spacing and what foundations to use.

The affective domain

The concept of the affective domain was developed by Krathwohl et al. (1964) and relates to the teaching of attitudes, values or beliefs. The levels in the affective domain range from receive (be willing to accept the beliefs and values stated) to internalise (acting in accordance with that set of values).

Attitudes to recycling are a particularly current example here. You may have been informed about the need to recycle and have started to think about it, speaking to your friends about whether they recycle and making a conscious decision to put your cans in the recycling bin instead of the general waste. Eventually, your recycling may become second nature and you do it without thinking.

If your teaching relates to the affective domain, you might consider using discussions, debates or role play. All of these methods encourage learners to consider other viewpoints, which is a key factor in changing attitudes.

Question

What kinds of subjects could be considered within the affective domain?

Answer

You might have considered subjects including health and safety or, within a range of other subjects, ethical considerations are often a requirement. You will find that teaching in the affective domain relates to elements of every course, examining learners' attitudes to subjects and even their behaviour. If you work to change learners' attitudes to classroom behaviour you are teaching in the affective domain.

Now that you know a little more about the different learning domains, you should be in a better position to distinguish between some of the active verbs used in each of the domains.

Question

Read through the list of active verbs below and decide which ones would be used with each learning domain.

build, analyse, draw, question, describe, list, paint, appreciate, listen, dance, evaluate, argue

Answer

Cognitive domain: *analyse, describe, list, evaluate*

Psychomotor domain: *build, draw, paint, dance*

Affective domain: *appreciate, listen, argue, question*

PLANNING FOR LEARNING SUPPORT

You may find that one (or more) of your learners has additional learning support needs and, as such, they will have a Learning Support Assistant (LSA) who will work with them in the classroom. You will need to spend time discussing your learner's needs with the LSA and you need to plan accordingly. The LSA will have a wide range of valuable knowledge in terms of meeting learners' individual needs and it is important that you take this on board as you plan your lesson, while at the same time giving clear direction about their role in helping you support the learner in achieving their objectives.

FUNCTIONAL AND WIDER SKILLS

While your subject-specialist knowledge is a core element of your practice when teaching in FE, this is not your only responsibility. In addition, you need to be able to support the development of learners' mathematics, English, ICT and wider skills that will aid them in their future lives and employment.

Government reports

The need for a workforce that has good mathematics and English skills was noted by the Leitch Report (2006). This report emphasised the need for many adults to develop their skills in literacy (English) and numeracy (mathematics) and made a bold target of aiming for 95 per cent of adults to have functional literacy and numeracy skills by 2020 in order to compete in a global market.

While learners may have specific functional skills classes aimed at helping them to achieve the required levels in each area, as a teacher, you should be able to make the most of opportunities that arise in your own classroom in order to help learners develop their skills in mathematics, English and ICT. By doing this and linking to your specialist area, you are not only developing learners' functional and wider skills, you are also making it clear that these play a key part in any future employment and contributing towards an attitude shift in them recognising the importance of these skills.

Embedding functional skills

Functional skills often fit easily with many subject areas. For example, learners on a travel and tourism course may be asked to use a computer to create a poster, thereby developing their ICT skills; calculate a holiday cost, developing mathematics skills or write a letter to a customer, developing their skills in written English. If you are incorporating these elements within a specialist area, rather than teaching them individually, you are *embedding* functional skills.

Question

Jane is teaching a vocational floristry course and is unsure how to embed functional skills in mathematics, English and ICT. Can you suggest ways in which she can do this?

Answer

There are many ways in which functional skills can be embedded in each subject area. To embed mathematics into a floristry class, you might have suggested that Jane could get the learners to create invoices, price items or even calculate profit. For English, you might have thought about communication skills, with Jane getting learners to use role play, with one learner playing a customer and another the florist. For ICT, Jane could get learners to create a spreadsheet or database and use it to record supplier information, sales figures or even to create invoices.

THE MINIMUM CORE

The Minimum Core refers to the minimum skills and knowledge in literacy and language, numeracy and ICT required by teachers in FE and forms an essential part of your development as a trainee teacher. While your learners need to develop their own functional skills in mathematics, English and ICT, as a teacher, you will also need to develop your own Minimum Core skills.

Each area of the Minimum Core comprises two parts:

o   Part A Knowledge and understanding

o   Part B Personal skills

Part A relates to your knowledge and understanding of each of the Minimum Core areas; for example, understanding how numeracy skills vary with age or the influence of gender and socio-economic factors. Part B relates to your practical application of your skills in each of the Minimum Core areas; for example, the effective communication of numeracy concepts or assessment of learners' understanding of numeracy.

Question

What do you understand by the term *socio-economic factors*?

Answer

Socio-economic factors usually refer to influences such as social class, family income and education. You will probably have learners from a range of socio-economic groups and the Minimum Core emphasises the need to be aware of the impact of various factors on your learners' motivation and how they learn.

You may already have strong *skills* in each of the Minimum Core areas – if you do, you have a head start, but you will see from the previous discussion that you also need to ensure that you develop your *knowledge and understanding* in relation to mathematics, English and ICT. Perhaps you have excellent mathematics skills, but have little knowledge of the factors that influence your learners' acquisition of mathematical skills. This would therefore be an area that you would need to develop as part of your own Minimum Core.

SUMMARY

As a teacher in FE, planning informs not only your delivery but everything that you do, helping to ensure that you meet the needs of your learners and your organisation. By developing your skills in preparing planning documentation, you can be clear about your learners' needs and what you want them to learn at each stage of their journey.

Planning and delivery will require that you consider wider needs, moving beyond those of your subject-specialist area to consider learners' skills and knowledge in mathematics, English and ICT and the essential skills that they will require to aid them in their future employment and everyday lives.

 Check your understanding

You will find some suggested answers at the back of this book.

Activity 1:   Explain in one sentence the difference between a teaching and learning plan and a scheme of work.

Activity 2:   What practical considerations do you need to consider when planning your scheme of work?

Activity 3:   Review the objectives that you have written on one of your teaching and learning plans. Can you make any changes to ensure that the objectives are SMART?

Activity 4:   Explain in one sentence the difference between aims and objectives.

Activity 5:   Why is *understand* not an acceptable verb to use when writing objectives?

Activity 6:   Consider the following lesson topics. What do you consider to be the primary learning domain?

   ○   appreciating a poem;

   ○   learning a language;

   ○   changing a tyre;

   ○   writing a story;

   ○   decorating a cake.

Activity 7:   What is meant by *embedding* functional skills?

Activity 8:   Suggest ways in which you can embed functional skills in mathematics, English and ICT into your own subject area.

Activity 9:   Explain in one sentence the difference between Minimum Core and functional skills.

Activity 10: Write down at least three factors that can influence the acquisition of learners' ICT skills.

End of chapter reflections: Outline five key points that you have learned from reading this chapter.

 TAKING IT FURTHER

In addition to the literature already commented upon in this chapter you may find the following literature of interest.

Gravells, A., and Simpson, S. (2010) *Planning and Enabling Learning in the Lifelong Learning Sector* (2nd edn). Exeter: Learning Matters.

Gronlund, N.E., and Brookhart, S.M. (2009) *Gronlund's Writing Instructional Objectives* (8th edn). Upper Saddle River, NJ: Pearson Education.

Ingleby, E., Joyce, D., and Powell, S. (2010) *Learning To Teach in the Lifelong Learning Sector*. London: Continuum.

Machin, L. (2009) *The Minimum Core for Language and Literacy*, Audit and Test. Exeter: Learning Matters.

Machin, L., Hindmarch, D., Richardson, T., Murray, S., (2014) *A Complete Guide to the Level 5 Diploma in Education and Training*, Northwich, Critical Publishing.

Murray, S. (2009) *The Minimum Core for ICT*, Audit and Test. Exeter: Learning Matters.

Patmore, M., and Woodhouse, S. (2009) *The Minimum Core For Numeracy*, Audit and Test. Exeter: Learning Matters.

REFERENCES

Bloom, B.S. (ed) (1956) *Taxonomy of Educational Objectives: The Classification of Educational Goals*. Handbook I: Cognitive Domain. New York: David McKay.

Dave, R.H. (1970) Psychomotor levels, in Armstrong, R.J. (ed) *Developing and Writing Educational Objectives* (pp33–34) Tucson, AZ: Educational Innovators Press.

ETF (2014) www.et-foundation.co.uk/ [accessed May 2015].

Krathwohl, D.R., Bloom B.S., and Masia, B.B. (1964) *Taxonomy of Educational Objectives: The Classification of educational Goals: Handbook II: The Affective Domain*. New York: David McKay.

Leitch, Lord S. (2006) *The Leitch Review of Skills: Prosperity for All in the Global Economy – World Class Skills*, Final Report. London: The Stationery Office.

Simpson, E. J. (1966) *The classification of educational objectives: Psychomotor domain*, *10*(4): 110–144.

8 Teaching practice and observations

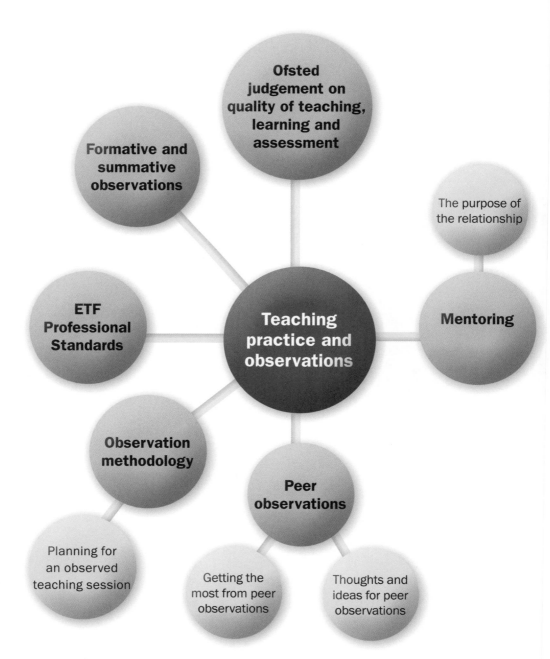

Ofsted judgement on quality of teaching, learning and assessment

Formative and summative observations

The purpose of the relationship

ETF Professional Standards

Teaching practice and observations

Mentoring

Observation methodology

Peer observations

Planning for an observed teaching session

Getting the most from peer observations

Thoughts and ideas for peer observations

KEY WORDS

ASCL, awarding organisations, ETF, LSIS, mentor, observations, observer, Ofsted, professional standards.

PROFESSIONAL LINKS

Your professional practice and observations are an essential part of your level 4 CET qualification. The idea of teaching practice and observations runs throughout all of the level 4 CET units and is covered in the following units in particular:

○ *Delivering education and training (level 4):*

○ *1.1, 1.2, 1.3; 2.1, 2.2, 2.3; 4.1, 4.2; 5.1, 5.2;*

○ *Assessing learners in education and training (level 4):*

○ *1.1, 1.2, 1.3, 1.4, 1.5; 2.1, 2.2, 2.3, 2.4, 2.5; 3.1, 3.2; 4.1, 4.2;*

○ *Using resources for education and training (level 4):*

○ *1.1, 1.2, 1.3; 2.1, 2.2; 3.1, 3.2.*

Specifically, this chapter also contributes to the following Professional Standards as provided by the Education and Training Foundation (ETF) (2014):

Professional values and attributes

1 Reflect on what works best in your teaching and learning to meet the diverse needs of learners

2 Evaluate and challenge your practice, values and beliefs

3 Inspire, motivate and raise aspirations of learners through your enthusiasm and knowledge

4 Be creative and innovative in selecting and adapting strategies to help learners to learn

5 Value and promote social and cultural diversity, equality of opportunity and inclusion

Professional knowledge and understanding

7 Maintain and update knowledge of your subject and/or vocational area

9 Apply theoretical understanding of effective practice in teaching, learning and assessment drawing on research and other evidence

10 Evaluate your practice with others and assess its impact on learning

11 Manage and promote positive learner behaviour

12 Understand the teaching and professional role and your responsibilities

Professional skills

13 Motivate and inspire learners to promote achievement and develop their skills to enable progression

14 Plan and deliver effective learning programmes for diverse groups or individuals in a safe and inclusive environment

15 Promote the benefits of technology and support learners in its use

16 Address the mathematics and English needs of learners and work creatively to overcome individual barriers to learning

17 Enable learners to share responsibility for their own learning and assessment, setting goals that stretch and challenge

18 Apply appropriate and fair methods of assessment and provide constructive and timely feedback to support progression and achievement

A list of all of the Standards can be found at the back of this book (Appendix 1).

INTRODUCTION

Observations, in particular, are often dreaded. No matter how experienced or inexperienced a teacher you are, this chapter seeks to help you to make the most of your professional practice and observations by helping you to be prepared and able to show your teaching and learning at its most effective. In this way, this chapter aims to meet the following objectives:

○ to help you prepare for observations of your professional practice;

○ to assist you in identifying the components of what makes a good lesson;

○ to support you in getting the most from your mentor and your professional practice.

STARTING POINT

What do you already know about teaching practice and observation?

○ What observations and teaching practice will you need to complete?

○ What do you consider the purpose of an observation to be?

○ What skills do you need in order to be an effective teacher?

○ Do you have access to teaching practice in different contexts and with learners at different levels?

This information is intended as a guideline only. The following information is taken from the Learning and Skills Improvement Service (LSIS) Guidance for Employers and Practitioners (LSIS, 2013). You must refer to your qualification handbook for specific requirements of teaching practice and observations for the level 4 CET qualification.

You are required to do 30 hours of practice for this qualification. You do not need to show evidence of working with groups unless units are undertaken which specify that purpose. However, where trainee teachers are working solely with individuals, a pro-gramme may also include support and preparation for working with groups.

LSIS (2013) believes that effective teaching practice experience should include:

○   different teaching practice locations/settings/contexts;

○   teaching across more than one level;

○   teaching a variety of learners;

○   teaching individuals and groups (if appropriate);

○   experience of non-teaching roles;

○   gaining subject-specialist knowledge through workplace mentoring.

You need to be observed a minimum of three times, totalling three hours (this excludes any observed practice completed as part of the level 3 Award in Education and Training). Any single observation must be a minimum of half an hour. The three observations must be linked to the following mandatory units:

○   Delivering education and training (level 4);

○   Assessing learners in education and training (level 4);

○   Using resources for education and training (level 4).

You need to make sure that your observations are appropriately spaced throughout the whole programme to take into account your progress. The awarding organisations (AOs) or HEIs will provide guidance to enable observers to make a judgement about whether a teacher has met the required standard of practice in an observation. LSIS (2013) recom-mends that awarding organisations refer to the *Handbook for the Inspection of Further Education and Skills*– Part 2, Section B: Quality of Teaching, Learning and Assessment (Ofsted, 2012) to inform the development of their guidance. Below is the information taken from the chapter on quality of teaching and learning, but the other chapters are just as important to you as a teacher.

OFSTED JUDGEMENT ON QUALITY OF TEACHING, LEARNING AND ASSESSMENT

Inspectors will make a judgement on the quality of teaching, learning and assessment by evaluating the extent to which:

○   learners benefit from high expectations, engagement, care, support and motivation from staff;

o   staff use their skills and expertise to plan and deliver teaching, learning and support to meet each learner's needs;

o   staff initially assess learners' starting points and monitor their progress, set challenging tasks, and build on and extend learning for all learners;

o   learners understand how to improve as a result of frequent, detailed and accurate feedback from staff following assessment of their learning;

o   teaching and learning develop English, mathematics and functional skills, and support the achievement of learning goals and career aims;

o   appropriate and timely information, advice and guidance support learning effectively;

o   equality and diversity are promoted through teaching and learning.

(Ofsted, 2012)

Question

Do you know when your organisation was last inspected by Ofsted?

Answer

If you do not know the answer to this (or even if you do) check with your organisation; also look at the information below for provision that is inspected by Ofsted.

Provision inspected under the Common Inspection Framework: the Common Inspection Framework (CIF) applies to the inspection of provision either wholly or partly funded by the Skills Funding Agency (SFA) or Education Funding Agency (EFA) in:

o   further education colleges, sixth-form colleges and independent specialist colleges;

o   independent learning providers: companies;

o   community learning and skills providers: local authorities, specialist designated institutions and not-for-profit organisations;

o   employers;

o   higher education institutions providing further education;

o   providers of learning in the judicial services.

The different types of provision inspected under the CIF for learners aged 16–18 and 19+, and learners aged 14–16 in colleges only, are:

o   apprenticeships, access to apprenticeships and National Vocational Qualifications (NVQs) offered in the workplace;

- ○ community learning;

- ○ National Careers Service – careers advice and guidance;

- ○ learning programmes leading to a qualification;

- ○ learning provision in the judicial services;

- ○ employability programmes;

- ○ foundation learning.

(Ofsted, 2012)

ETF PROFESSIONAL STANDARDS

As well as Ofsted guidelines for teaching and learning, there are also the ETF's Professional Standards for Teachers and Trainers in Education and Training – England. These (as outlined in the historical backdrop to FE in the Introduction to this book) were written in 2014 and replaced the LLUK's New Overarching Standards for Teachers, Tutors and Trainers in the Lifelong Learning Sector.

The standards sit within three domains as listed below:

- ○ professional values and attributes;

- ○ professional knowledge and understanding;

- ○ Professional skills.

There are 20 standards that sit within these domains. These standards are listed in Appendix 1.

Question

How many of the above standards are applicable to you as a teacher?

Answer

All of them.

OBSERVATION METHODOLOGY

Your qualification paperwork may well include a pre-observation checklist. If not, then the following quick checklist can be used to help make sure that you are prepared for an observation.

Table 8.1 Pre-observation checklist

Have you made contact with your observer?	
If this is your first observation, do you feel that you understand the observation process? If you do not, please talk to your observer or course tutor.	
If this is not your first observation, do you have the feedback from your previous observation to reflect upon and use for your next observation?	
Do you have a spare copy of your paperwork and resources to give to your observer (eg lesson plan, scheme of work, sample individual learning plans (ILPs) and resources)?	
Do you have time and a quiet place to receive feedback on your observed session?	
If you do not have time and a quiet place to receive feedback on the observed session, have you let the observer know so that arrangements can be made to feedback as soon as possible after the observed session?	
Are you spacing your observations out over the academic year?	
Are you completing your reflective journal regularly?	
Have you decided how you are going to introduce the observer to your class?	
Are you familiar with the Ofsted and ETF Professional Standards against which your observation may be assessed?	
Make sure that you have clarified with the observer where you are going to meet (reception, classroom, etc.)	

Planning for an observed teaching session

Before the lesson:

o   do you have a scheme of work and teaching and learning plan that is appropriate for the needs of the learners (individuals and group) and the subject?

o   do you have access to all of the resources needed for that lesson, including any extension activities?

o   is any technical equipment needed working and do you have a back-up plan for any failure of technical equipment?

o   does the room layout need changing?

At the beginning of the lesson:

o   take the register and remember to record any latecomers as they arrive;

o   challenge latecomers, as appropriate;

o   recap the topic from the previous lesson;

○ make sure learners understand what the learning outcomes are for that lesson – is it appropriate to have the learning outcomes written down for the learners?

In the lesson:

○ use activities that are interesting and suit learners' needs in terms of ability;

○ get the learners actively engaged in the learning;

○ make sure that the learners understand how what you are teaching them fits into their vocational or academic area and how it can be used in their everyday lives;

○ give the learners clear instructions about what they should be doing in each part of the lesson, including assessment strategies;

○ vary assessment strategies, including self-assessment and peer assessment, where appropriate;

○ make sure the learners' individual needs are catered for and all learners are engaged in the learning;

○ support literacy, numeracy and language where appropriate;

○ use age-appropriate, inclusive resources, including ICT, where appropriate;

○ give feedback within the lesson (written and verbal);

○ be aware of any inappropriate behaviour or language.

Towards the end of the lesson:

○ go back and check that learning outcomes have been met;

○ ask or perhaps get the learners to write down what they have learned;

○ check to see if any elements are still outstanding and need to be carried over to the next lesson;

○ if you are giving out homework, make sure it is clearly set;

○ explain to students what you are going to cover in the next lesson and how it fits in with what has been done in that lesson.

At the end of the lesson:

○ gain verbal feedback as soon as possible from your observer;

○ reflect on the lesson, using your own feedback as well as your observer's;

○ write a reflection based on the lesson (you will find information about how to reflect in Chapter 1);

○ discuss the lesson, feedback and reflection with your mentor;

○ build on any developmental aspects for your next lesson and your next observation.

FORMATIVE AND SUMMATIVE OBSERVATIONS

Some of your observations on your course may be summative and some may be formative. First of all, look at Chapter 4 to understand the difference between formative and summative assessments. In the context of observations, formative ones allow you to develop your teaching skills without having to worry if you have passed or failed your observation, while summative observations will have pass/fail criteria to them. Some courses grade the observations using the CIF (CIF, 2012).

Table 8.2 Common Inspection Framework (2012)

Grade 1	Outstanding
Grade 2	Good
Grade 3	Requires improvement (used to be satisfactory)
Grade 4	Inadequate

Others may use the CIF language rather than the grades. Coffield (2012) believes that grading should be abolished in the FE sector as he feels it can be very damaging, with teachers graded at a 3 or 4 only focusing on the grade and ignoring any comments. Similarly, teachers graded at grade 1 or 2 feel pressure immediately to keep getting a 1 or 2. A bad teacher can have a good observation and a good teacher can have an off-day and a bad observation. Coffield (2012) therefore feels that observations should be seen as a continuing process rather than a one-off where someone managed to hit the right number on the right day.

Some observers use a simple pass/fail, while others use a system for differentiating between a bare pass and a very good pass by using: good, very good and excellent or pass, merit and distinction. Whatever you get, there is always room for reflection and development and, as Coffield (2012) says, should be seen in the context of your teaching, not as a one-off.

 Case study 1

Getting the most out of an observation

Emma has been working at a local FE college for three years. She completed a Preparing to Teach in the Lifelong Learning Sector (PTLLS) in her first year of teaching and has just enrolled on the level 4 qualification. She has been observed a couple of times as part of her job. These have been monitoring observations to make sure her teaching is appropriate but have provided no developmental opportunities for progression. Emma teaches ICT part time and hates being observed as she feels that if she does not do very well she will be sacked. Her last workplace observation was particularly stressful because the college IT system went down just as her lesson started and she did not have anything prepared for this contingency.

Emma is similarly dreading her first observation on her qualification. Before the observation, Emma runs through a pre-observation checklist and makes sure that she is ready for the observation. She meets the observer before the lesson and gives him her paperwork, including scheme of work, teaching and learning plan and the resources she is going to use in the lesson. She has also included a pen portrait of the students in her class and any needs that they have that have been built into the lesson.

During the lesson, Emma followed the structure of the teaching and learning plan, deviating only when it suited the best needs of the learners – where she could give a coherent explanation of her reason for moving away from the teaching and learning plan to the observer. At the end of the lesson she found a quiet space for her and the observer to discuss the lesson. The observer asked her to reflect on the lesson and through questioning allowed Emma to discuss the elements of the class that went well and those she was less satisfied with, helping Emma to come up with some developmental areas to work on in her teaching and learning.

After the observation, once Emma had received the written feedback from the observer, she had a meeting with her mentor and they came up with a written reflection on the lesson and an action plan. Emma then carried those ideas into her lessons and was able to then review her reflection. In this way, Emma felt in control of the lesson observation and was able to develop her teaching and learning in a non-judgemental way.

PEER OBSERVATIONS

Peer observations are undertaken when you observe someone who is at the same level (has a similar job role) as you and they then have the opportunity to observe you. They are not meant to be hierarchical observations. However, peer observations can sometimes be an opportunity for an inexperienced teacher to observe and be observed by an experienced teacher. Or two experienced teachers might be paired together to help them reflect on their own way of teaching and other ways of going about teaching and learning. You may be able to choose who you peer observe or have the choice made for you. You may be undertaking peer observations as part of your course or your organisation may undertake yearly peer observations anyway. Whatever the reason, the tips and hints below can help you to get the most from your peer observations.

Getting the most from peer observations

Peer observations can be seen as a complete waste of time or a valuable way of sharing good practice, resources and ideas – depending on how you approach them. There is really very little point in observing a good friend, who you already share resources with and know their teaching style. The feedback is unlikely to contribute to any significant developmental suggestions. Similarly, going along to a peer observation with a closed mind determined to hate whatever you see might mean that you are missing a valuable opportunity to help both of you develop.

Thoughts and ideas for peer observations

○ Are there set criteria that you are supposed to observe against or a proforma to complete?

○ Do you have copies of paperwork for an observation – such as teaching and learning plan, scheme of work?

○ Take time out of the peer observation to look at another teacher's resources and websites that they regularly use.

○ Are you clear on the learning outcomes and how they are going to be assessed?

○ Take time to verbally feedback as well as more formally in writing – begin a professional dialogue about the teaching that you might want to continue.

○ Suggest ideas: don't be overly critical, but be constructive. Remember that what goes around, comes around.

○ Peer observations are a two-way process, you can learn both from observing and being observed.

○ You might suggest an area of your teaching and learning that you would particularly like your observer to focus on.

○ Professional discussions should remain confidential. You should not talk about someone else's teaching in a derogatory manner; if you have any concerns then talk confidentially to your line manager.

○ Each peer observation should consist of three meetings: first to discuss the context of the teaching before the observation, the second meeting is the observation, and the third meeting is a dialogue about the observation.

 Case study 2

The General Secretary of the Association of Schools and College Leaders (ASCL) completed an interview in IfL's summer 2012 edition of *InTuition*, their in-house magazine, in which he talked about the value of peer observations. He mentioned that when he was a newly qualified teacher he asked if he could conduct a peer observation on another teacher. He particularly wanted to improve his skills in keeping students engaged and on task. He felt that he learned more in one hour of observing a peer and having a discussion afterwards than he could have done on any course and he has been convinced of the value of peer observations ever since.

(Lightman, 2012)

Question

Why might the General Secretary in the case study above have learned more than he would have done by attending a course?

Answer

Peer observations provide a valuable opportunity to see another person teaching as well as being able to observe learners' responses. As teachers often work in their classrooms isolated from other teachers, the CET qualification provides an excellent opportunity to observe others and to get feedback on your own teaching.

MENTORING

At the start of your course you will probably be asked to name a person in your organisation who will be your mentor in the workplace for the duration of the course. The mentor will need to be a current – or recent – subject specialist (within your relevant subject area). If there is no one appropriate in your workplace, let your course tutor know as soon as possible. The mentor may well be chosen for you. You need to be able to be open and honest with your mentor and feel that you can confide in them without it jeopardising your job. For these reasons, it might be better not to have your line manager mentor you as the lines between the different roles can become blurred.

The purpose of the relationship

The mentoring relationship can take a number of forms.

○ Your mentor could give advice and help you with your reflective journal.

○ Your mentor could support 'areas for self-development' outlined in feedback from formative and summative observations, to ensure that formal observations are used effectively and you make progress.

○ Your mentor can help to link theory and practice in the workplace.

○ The mentor could be observed by the mentee.

○ The mentor could observe the mentee as part of a formative or summative observation.

Really it is the mentee who should be setting the agenda for what is addressed in the mentoring lessons; they should be seen far more as coaching lessons than teaching lessons. A mentor's place is not to say: *this is what you are doing wrong... this is what I would do...* Many mentors have been on mentoring training. If they have not, your course may provide advice and guidance to help them mentor you.

> *Mentoring relates primarily to the identification and nurturing of potential for the whole person; it can be a long term relationship, where the goals may change but are always set by the learner. The learner owns both the goals and the process.*
>
> (Megginson and Clutterbuck, 2006, p232)

SUMMARY

Question

Which Standards do you think your current roles and responsibilities as a teacher cover? Refer to the ETF Professional *Standards* for guidance (the address is provided in the *References* section at the end of this chapter).

 Check your understanding

You will find suggested answers to some of these questions at the back of the book.

Activity 1: Note down two items that you think might be included in each of the ETF (2014) sections. Check the document to see if they are mentioned. Their website address is at the end of this chapter.

Activity 2: If your organisation or your course does not expect you to carry out peer observations, organise an informal peer observation with a colleague or suggest to your line manager that it might be a good idea for your department to instigate them.

Activity 3: Find out if there are any differences in how you will be observed for the purpose of the level 4 CET qualification and for the purpose of your organisation's quality assurance process.

Activity 4: What paperwork do you need to show your mentor?

Activity 5: How often should you and your mentor meet?

Activity 6: Does your mentor have to observe you teaching and do you have to observe your mentor?

Activity 7: Do you have to have a mentor?

End of chapter reflections: Outline five key points that you have learned from reading this chapter.

 TAKING IT FURTHER

In addition to the literature already commented upon in this chapter, you may find the following websites of interest.

Coaching Network: www.coachingnetwork.org.uk [accessed January 2015].

Excellence Gateway: www.excellencegateway.org.uk/ [accessed January 2015].

REFERENCES

CIF (2012) *Common Inspection Framework for Further Education and Skills*. [online]. Available at: www.ofsted.gov.uk/resources/common-inspection-framework-for-further-education-and-skills-2012 [accessed January 2015].

Coffield, F. (2012) To grade or not to grade? *Adults Learning*, Spring 2012: 38–39. [online. Available at: www.niace.org.uk/sites/default/files/documents/adults-learning/AdultsLearning_2012_04-pages38-39.pdf [accessed January 2015].

ETF (2014) Professional Standards for Teachers and Trainers in Education and Training. [online]. Available at: www.et-foundation.co.uk [accessed January 2015].

FEDA (1999) *FENTO Standards for Teaching and Learning*. London: FEDA.

Lightman, B. (2012) Let's stay focused on lesson observations. *InTuition*, 9: 8. [Online]. Available at; www.ifl.ac.uk/__data/assets/pdf_file/0008/27890/InTuition-issue-9-Summer-2012.pdf [accessed January 2015].

LLUK (2007) *New Overarching Professional Standards for Teachers, Tutors and Trainers in the Lifelong Learning Sector*. [Online]. Available at: collections.europarchive.org/tna/20110214161207/http:/www.lluk.org/wp-content/uploads/2010/11/new-overarching-standards-for-ttt-in-lifelong-learning-sector.pdf [accessed January 2015].

LSIS (2013) *Teaching and Training Qualifications for the Further Education and Skills Sector in England, Guidance for Employers and Practitioners*. [online]. Available at: www.lsis.org.uk/publication-content/teaching-and-training-qualifications-further-education-and-skills-sector-england [accessed January 2015].

Megginson, D and Clutterbuck, D. (2006) Creating a Coaching Culture. *Industrial and Commercial Training*, 38(5): 232–37.

Ofsted (2012) *Handbook for the Inspection of Further Education and Skills – Part 2, Section B: Quality of Teaching, Learning and Assessment*. [online]. Available at: www.national-training.com/Handbook-Inspection-FE-and-Skills-Sept-2012.pdf [accessed January 2015].

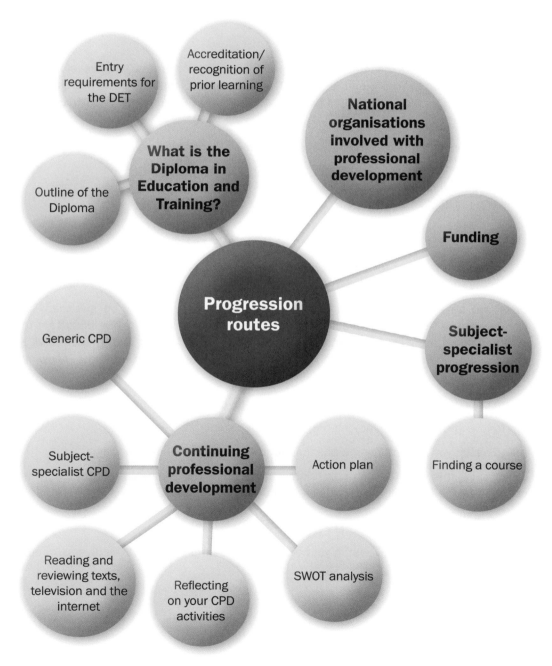

KEY WORDS

action plan, APL, ATLS, CPD, Commission on Adult Vocational Teaching and Learning (CAVTL), DfE, Diploma in Education and Training (DET), DTLLS, ESOL, ETF, occupational competence progression, PGCE, QCF, QTLS, reflection, RPL, SWOT analysis.

PROFESSIONAL LINKS

This chapter considers the importance of effective continuing professional development (CPD) in your own teaching and learning. The concept and importance of professional development runs throughout all of the level 4 Certificate CET units and in particular the following units:

○ *Planning to meet the needs of learners in education and training (level 4):*
   1.1, 1.2, 1.3; 2.1, 2.2, 2.3, 2.4, 2.5; 3.1, 3.2; 4.1, 4.2.

○ *Delivering education and training (level 4):*
   1.1, 1.2, 1.3; 2.1, 2.2, 2.3; 3.1, 3.2; 4.1, 4.2; 5.1, 5.2.

○ *Assessing learners in education and training (level 4):*
   1.1, 1.2, 1.3, 1.4, 1.5; 2.1, 2.2, 2.3, 2.4, 2.5; 3.1, 3.2; 4.1, 4.2.

○ *Using resources for education and training (level 4):*
   1.1, 1.2, 1.3; 2.1, 2.2; 3.1, 3.2.

Once you have completed your level 4 CET qualification, you may be given advice from your tutor about other qualifications that you could move on to. It is important to give this some thought before embarking on another qualification and to seek advice about possible progression routes. In this way, this chapter aims to meet the following objectives:

○ to provide you with information about higher level teacher training courses;

○ to give you support in making progression decisions;

○ to assist you in identifying areas for your own professional development.

Specifically, this chapter also contributes to the following Professional Standards as provided by the Education and Training Foundation (ETF) (2014):

Professional values and attributes

1   Reflect on what works best in your teaching and learning to meet the diverse needs of learners

Professional knowledge and understanding

7   Maintain and update knowledge of your subject and/or vocational area

8   Maintain and update your knowledge of educational research to develop evidence-based practice

9   Apply theoretical understanding of effective practice in teaching, learning and assessment drawing on research and other evidence

10 Evaluate your practice with others and assess its impact on learning

Professional skills

19 Maintain and update your teaching and training expertise and vocational skills through collaboration with employers

20 Contribute to organisational development and quality improvement through collaboration with others

A list of all of the Standards can be found at the back of this book (Appendix 1).

STARTING POINT

Where are you now and where do you want to go?

○   What were your goals and aspirations before you enrolled onto the level 4 CET qualification?

○   What are you current goals and aspirations?

○   What do you need to do in order to achieve these goals and aspirations?

INTRODUCTION

The level 4 CET qualification is a medium-sized qualification suitable for teachers or trainee teachers who want a qualification that focuses on practical teaching and who are ready to study at the same level as the first year of a degree.

Once you have completed this qualification, you may be given advice about how to progress on to a higher level or longer qualification. This is not a quick decision to make. A starting point would be to consult a line manager at work to find out what progression route your workplace would like you to follow, as there may be a difference between your workplace progression and your own preferred professional development. For example, your workplace may want you to complete a qualification so you can be asked to work in a different area of teaching and learning. Although this may not be an area you had thought to move into, it might help to make your position more secure, so it is worth thinking about. Make the most of a meeting with a line manager about progression by reading through this chapter and doing research beforehand.

WHAT IS THE DIPLOMA IN EDUCATION AND TRAINING?

The progression route upwards from a level 4 CET would be to undertake the level 5 Diploma in Education and Training (DET) qualification. This is a larger qualification for teachers or trainee teachers who want to or who have an extensive range of training responsibilities and are ready to study at the same level as the second year of a degree course. A level 5 teaching qualification is the level that is recommended at a national level as a suitable qualification for teachers in adult education to aspire to.

The level 5 DET was a new qualification for the academic year 2013–14. It was devised by LSIS after a review of the teacher training qualifications as requested by the government. The DET qualification replaced the DTLLS. The DTLLS was a fairly new qualification, only available since 2007, which replaced the qualifications that many may be familiar with: the Certificate in Education and Postgraduate Certificate in Education (PGCE) – Further and Adult Education.

Awarding organisations such as City and Guilds have to use the QCF qualification titles (further information about the QCF can be found in the Introduction). However, HEIs do not have to use the QCF titles, so you may find the new level 5 qualification offered by universities is still called the Certificate in Education or the Postgraduate Certificate of Education for Adult Education. All of this can be very confusing but the qualification you will be looking for is the equivalent of the DET.

Outline of the Diploma

The information for this section is taken from the LSIS document: *Teaching and Training Qualifications for the Further Education and Skills Sector in England: Guidance for Employers and Practitioners* (LSIS, 2013), which would be a good document for you to look at when thinking about doing higher level teaching qualifications.

The DET is for people who hold or want to hold a teaching role with an extensive range of teaching or training responsibilities, including those in more than one context. To be awarded the level 5 DET qualification, a total of 120 credits must be achieved. There is also a requirement for a minimum of 100 hours of teaching practice.

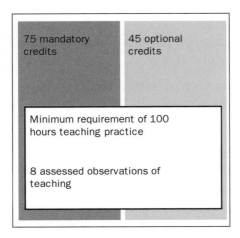

75 mandatory credits

45 optional credits

Minimum requirement of 100 hours teaching practice

8 assessed observations of teaching

Figure 9.1 Requirements for the level 5 Diploma

The mandatory units cover:

- planning, delivering and evaluating inclusive learning and teaching;
- assessing learning in education and training;
- understanding theories, principles and models in education and training;
- understanding professionalism and the influence of professional values in education and training.

There are also optional units that offer action research, understanding and managing behaviours in a learning environment, literacy or numeracy theories and frameworks, and engaging with employers. A full list of the optional units available can be found at the end of these chapters.

Entry requirements for the DET

If you want to progress by taking the level 5 DET qualification, you need to have 100 hours of teaching practice and be able to be observed 8 times. You will need to undertake an initial assessment of skills in English, mathematics and ICT and follow an action plan to improve those skills, if necessary.

However, a provider of initial teacher training can set their own entry requirements above the level of the national requirements, and many of them request that a teacher entering a level 5 teaching qualification already have a level 3 qualification in the area in which they teach and be able to demonstrate that they already have level 2 skills in literacy and numeracy. Therefore it is imperative to check the entry requirements of the local provider.

Accreditation/recognition of prior learning

Trainee teachers who have achieved the level 4 Certificate in Education and Training can transfer twenty hours of practice and two hours of observed and assessed practice towards the practice requirements for the level 5 Diploma in Education and Training (LSIS, 2013).

This means that if you go on to study the level 5 DET qualification after completing the level 4 CET qualification you will only have to show 80 hours of practice and to have 6 of your teaching sessions observed. Again, you will need to speak to the provider of the qualification about any APL/RPL being applied to you.

SUBJECT-SPECIALIST PROGRESSION

It may be that you are interested in completing a subject-specialist course as well as a DET qualification. It is possible to do these qualifications as a specialist (integrated) or separate courses.

The specialist qualifications are:

- level 5 Diploma in Education and Training (including teaching English: ESOL);
- level 5 Diploma in Education and Training (including teaching English: Literacy);

- level 5 Diploma in Education and Training (including teaching English: Literacy and ESOL);

- level 5 Diploma in Education and Training (including teaching Mathematics: Numeracy);

- level 5 Diploma in Education and Training (including teaching Disabled Learners).

Again, an HEI may call the qualifications by different names, so it is worth checking or requesting an interview to make sure that you are enrolling on the qualification that is appropriate for you. So, at the end of one of these qualifications, you would have a level 5 Diploma and a subject specialism as well. This may help you to find employment and teaching hours in areas such as Functional Skills or special needs. Check the entry requirements for these courses, as a level 3 qualification in English or mathematics may well be necessary.

Finding a course

There are a number of different kinds of organisation that offer the level 5 DET qualification, including universities, colleges and private training organisations.

LSIS (2013) suggests the following advice for sources of information for finding a course:

- employers of teachers and trainers who may offer the qualifications in-house for their own staff;

- employers of teachers and trainers who may have a list of initial teacher training providers offering teaching qualifications in the local area;

- initial teacher training providers, many of whom will have websites that detail the courses on offer;

- awarding organisations, professional bodies and subject associations;

- Union learning representatives;

- FE Advice: www.feadvice.org.uk/next-steps

The TALENT website, www.talent.ac.uk, is also a good starting point to find subject-specialist courses; TALENT stands for training adult literacy, ESOL and numeracy teachers but it lists generic courses as well as specialist ones.

Question

Do you know what level 5 DET courses are available in your area and what the entry requirements are?

FUNDING

It is difficult to give advice about funding for qualifications as this can change very quickly. Your own organisation might run the courses and waive your fees or may be prepared to pay for you to attend elsewhere. You may find that the payment of fees by your organisation is dependent on you staying with them for a set amount of time (typically two or three years) at the end of the course, otherwise you will be asked to repay the fees. Make sure you are happy with this situation before embarking on a course.

There may be national funding for qualifications, golden hellos or bursaries, or there may be funding through student loans. It is worth finding out from your organisation about funding and visit the following websites for advice or information:

○   FE Advice: www.feadvice.org.uk/next-steps/funding-information;

○   Student Finance: www.gov.uk/student-finance;

○   The Education and Training Foundation: www.et-foundation.co.uk

---

 Case study 1

What next?

Priya is 40 years old. She works in an FE college and currently teaches hairdressing at level 1 and 2 after working in a salon for many years. She has just completed her level 4 CET qualification. She also has a level 4 qualification in Hairdressing and Barbering. As well as teaching at the college, Priya has to visit local salons, where she has apprentices working, in order to carry out work-based assessments. To help with the assessments, Priya has already been asked by her college to complete an A1 Assessors Award, which she has done.

As part of the apprenticeship scheme, Priya used to deliver Key Skills: Application of Number. With the transition to Functional Skills, Priya is now teaching Functional Skills: Mathematics to her apprentices and vocational learners.

Priya consulted her line manager about further qualifications and he decided the best qualification for her was the level 5 Diploma in Education and Training (Mathematics: Numeracy) qualification. This would give Priya a level 5 teaching qualification and a subject specialism in mathematics, which the government is recommending as a suitable qualification to teach Functional Skills. Priya already had an English and a Mathematics GCSE, both at grade C. To enrol on the level 5 Diploma in Education and Training (Mathematics: Numeracy) at the local university Priya had to prove that she could operate at level 3 in mathematics. She did this by completing a mathematics test prior to being enrolled on to the qualification.

Priya's college was unwilling to fund Priya on the course, but they were prepared to give her time off to attend. Priya contacted Student Finance England and applied for a tuition fee loan. This is a repayable loan that Priya will start paying back once she has finished her course. She will start paying it back immediately because she earns over £21,000 per annum. Each month she will repay 9 per cent of any income over £21,000. If her income dips below £21,000 then she will stop repayments.

When the qualification is completed, the level 5 Diploma in Education and Training with the integrated subject specialism of mathematics will mean that Priya is a specialist in two teaching areas.

CONTINUING PROFESSIONAL DEVELOPMENT

Continuing professional development (CPD) is well named, as it is continuous and should be undertaken throughout your teaching career. If you have decided to have a break before embarking on another significant qualification, this should not mean a break from all CPD. Be aware of any opportunities for CPD in your workplace as well as external CPD events. Finding out what organisations your workplace is a member of can be helpful because there are often significant discounts on events for members, a good bargaining point when requesting your workplace pay for you to attend an external event.

Before putting your name down for an event, ask yourself a number of questions:

- Is this training at the right level for me?
- Is it aimed at practitioners?
- Are there positive reviews for previous training sessions provided by this organisation?
- When you have completed the training ask yourself:
- What am I going to do with this training?
- How am I going to record this training event (see below for an action plan)?

There are two kinds of CPD event you could attend, generic CPD and subject-specialist CPD. The ETF (2014) states that all teachers in this sector should be regarded as dual professionals: expert in own area of teaching and also in teaching and learning itself. Your CPD choices need to reflect that dual professional role.

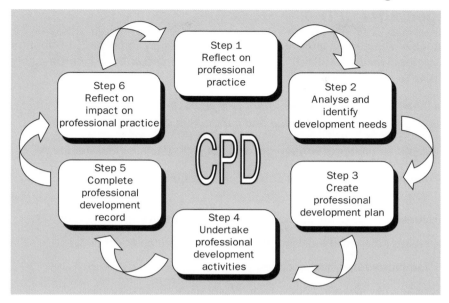

Figure 9.2 IfL's (2009) model of the CPD process

Generic CPD

This is professional development that applies to your generic teaching and learning skills. The following kinds of activities to update your teaching and learning skills:

○ mentoring and coaching new colleagues;

○ peer observation;

○ work shadowing;

○ team-teaching;

○ chairing and leading meetings;

○ carrying out and disseminating action research;

○ designing innovative curricula and feedback mechanisms.;

○ being involved in self-assessment processes

○ engaging in learning conversations with colleagues;

○ being an active member of a committee, board, or steering groups related to teaching and/or your subject area;

○ peer visits to community organisations/partners;

Subject-specialist CPD

CPD in your specialist teaching area is becoming increasingly important, to *confirm occupational competence* (LLUK, 2007). The Commission on Adult Vocational Teaching and Learning (CAVTL, 2013) advises:

Vocational teaching, learning and assessment is a sophisticated professional occupation and demands, therefore, robust initial and continuous development of expertise.

ETF (2014) suggests a number of ways to develop subject-specialist knowledge:

- ○ gaining further qualifications in your subject or industrial expertise through accredited courses;
- ○ industrial updating through visits, placements, secondments or shadowing;
- ○ being a member of a special interest group or another professional body;
- ○ taking on examiner/verifier/assessor responsibilities;
- ○ attending briefings by awarding bodies and disseminate to colleagues;
- ○ giving a presentation at a conference in your subject area;
- ○ supervising research;
- ○ subject learning coaching/training;
- ○ leading project development in your subject area;
- ○ writing reports/papers to inform your colleagues;
- ○ planning or running a staff development activity or event;
- ○ organising trips/ residential /work placements.

Reading and reviewing texts, television and the internet

Reading books, journals and getting involved in activities online can be an excellent way to be engaged in CPD. Keep a log of this kind of activity in the same way that you would an event you have attended and reflect on it and recommend it to colleagues as well. When completing an application form, it is good to list recent reading as well as actual CPD events.

If you do engage in professional discussions online: forums, Twitter, blogs, etc. remember to practise e-safety and never write anything online that you would not like your senior managers to read; once something is on the internet, it is virtually impossible to delete it.

Although Teachers TV is no longer active, the DfE has signed non-exclusive distribution agreements that means the archive will still be available online. A list of websites that stream the 15-minute clips is available – see *Taking It Further* at the end of this chapter. Teachers TV was created for schools but it can also be used for your own professional development, such as how to write learning outcomes to using in the classroom with your own students.

Reflecting on your CPD activities

At the end of most CPD events, the organisers ask you to complete a questionnaire of some kind asking for your feedback. They may also ask you to reflect on the impact it may have on your teaching and learning. This is a good exercise, but you then usually have to hand the information in. Therefore it is good practice for you to have some kind of form of your own that you can fill in and reflect on the training for you to keep in your CPD folder as a reminder of any action points needed to be carried out. It is vital that you reflect on the training to maximise its impact on your teaching and learning. As discussed in Chapter 1, it is important that you reflect on any CPD to see how any new skills and knowledge can be used to improve or to extend your abilities as a teacher. You will find a CPD template at the end of these chapters (Appendix 4), which will help you to focus on the actions that you have already taken as well as those that you need to plan for.

Your organisation may well keep a record of your CPD activities; however, it is always a good idea to keep your own up-to-date folder (or e-folder) of CPD activity. It is then easily accessible when planning more CPD or if you are applying for another teaching position.

 Case study 2

David is 32 years old and works for a private training organisation delivering work-based training to people in the care industry. He previously worked in the care industry and has a level 3 qualification in Health and Social care. He works one-to-one with learners employed as carers in the local area. In the last academic year he completed the level 4 CET qualification. He is due to have an annual review with his line manager and wanted to review some of his options for professional development before the meeting.

SWOT analysis

In the case study above, David should consider and make an analysis of his strengths, weaknesses, opportunities and threats. This is generally referred to as a SWOT analysis.

The process of a SWOT analysis can be very helpful in determining what you need to do and how best to do it in order to meet your aims, objectives, goals and aspirations.

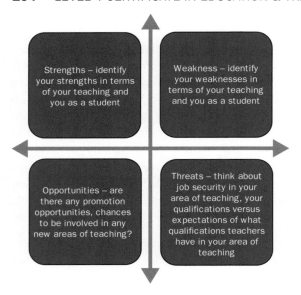

Figure 9.3 Outline of a SWOT analysis

When undertaking a SWOT analysis you should consider:

○   what are your professional development needs?

○   what actions need to be taken in order to meet these needs?

○   what resources will be required?

○   who do I need to go to for help and advice?

○   how am I going to use this professional development?

In the case study example above, David could consider the following:

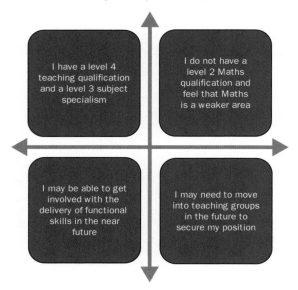

Figure 9.4 David's SWOT analysis

Action plan

Once David has established some general thoughts about his development he should then draw up an action plan.

Table 9.1 Example action plan

Professional development needs	Action to be taken	Resources and help needed	Timescale	How am I going to use this professional development?
Update on Functional Skills and delivery	Attend a national Functional Skills update and internal professional development on delivery of Functional Skills	Ask line manager's permission to attend	Next three months	
Complete a level 2 Mathematics qualification	Enrol on a level 2 Mathematics qualification within own college	Ask line manager's permission to attend and find a colleague who will agree to be Mathematics mentor Will college waive course fees?	Complete by end of academic year	
Support transition to group teaching	Find opportunities to teach groups in college with support and access internal professional development	Make sure to check intranet for professional development opportunities as not in college very often. Ask line manager to act as mentor and support group teaching opportunities	Over academic year	

> *Question*
>
> How can the skills and knowledge that you have gained during your time undertaking the level 4 CET qualification help you progress to a higher level qualification?

NATIONAL ORGANISATIONS INVOLVED WITH PROFESSIONAL DEVELOPMENT

One of the strands of the ETF is to oversee professional standards and qualifications and to help to support outstanding teaching and learning, leadership and management. The Foundation may well be a good place to start when looking for news on support for CPD and any funding opportunities that may be available for teacher training. The ETF took over this role in 2014 from the IFL and also took over membership from the IfL. As part of the membership a CPD resource and an online way of capturing professional development is available. At the moment, the ETF can also confer ATLS or QTLS status on a member who has the necessary qualifications. This is also known as professional formation so you can gain recognition and share good practice. There is a monetary cost to go through the process of professional formation. The process involves building a portfolio of evidence to show that you have appropriate qualifications to be regarded as fully qualified. There are two levels: ATLS, which stands for Associate Teacher of Learning and Skills, which you would be able to apply for with a level 4 qualification, and QTLS, Qualified Teacher of Learning and Skills, for which you would need a level 5 teaching qualification and at least a level 3 subject-specialist qualification.

SUMMARY

Developing your skills as a teacher is an on-going requirement throughout your career. Seek out opportunities to do this, remain current in your specialist subject, develop and update your technical skills and retain an interest in your area of teaching and the sector in which you work.

 # Check your understanding

Activity 1: Think about a CPD event you have recently attended and complete the CPD template at the back of this book (Appendix 4). Ensure that you carry out any action points you identify. If you have not attended any CPD events recently then look back at the model of the CPD process and complete the first three steps. Then see if there are opportunities for you to attend internal or external events to help complete your professional development plan.

Activity 2: Complete a SWOT analysis based on where you are now and where you would like to be in three years' time. Use the reflective techniques outlined in Chapter 1 to help you complete the SWOT analysis. Once you have completed the SWOT analysis, complete a professional development plan to either overcome weaknesses and threats or capitalise on strengths and opportunities. Again, think reflectively when completing the action plan and use the CPD template (Appendix 4) at the back of this book.

End of chapter reflections: Outline five key points that you have learned from reading this chapter.

 TAKING IT FURTHER

In addition to the literature already commented upon in this chapter you may find the following websites of interest.

Excellence Gateway: www.excellencegateway.org.uk [accessed January 2015].

Commission on Adult Vocational Teaching and Learning: www.excellencegateway.org. uk/cavtl [accessed January 2015].

Student Finance: www.gov.uk/student-finance [accessed January 2015].

Teachers TV: https://www.gov.uk/government/publications/teachers-tv/teachers-tv [accessed January 2015].

REFERENCES

CAVTL (2013) *Commission on Adult Vocational Teaching and Learning*, http://cavtl. excellencegateway.org.uk [accessed July 2015].

ETF (2014) Professional Standards for Teachers and Trainers in Education and Training. [online]. Available at: www.et-foundation.co.uk [accessed January 2015].

IfL (2009) *Guidelines for Your Continuing Professional Development*, www.ifl.ac.uk/__ data/assets/pdf_file/0011/5501/J11734-IfL-CPD-Guidelines-08.09-web-v3.pdf [accessed January 2015].

LLUK (2007) *New Overarching Professional Standards for Teachers, Tutors and Trainers in the Lifelong Learning Sector*. [online]. Available at: http://collections. europarchive.org/tna/20110214161207/http://www.lluk.org/wp-content/ uploads/2010/11/new-overarching-standards-for-ttt-in-lifelong-learning-sector. pdf [accessed January 2015].

LSIS (2013) *Teaching and Training Qualifications for the Further Education and Skills Sector in England: Guidance for Employers and Practitioners*. [online]. Available at: www.lsis.org.uk/publication-content/teaching-and-training-qualifications- further-education-and-skills-sector-england [accessed January 2015].

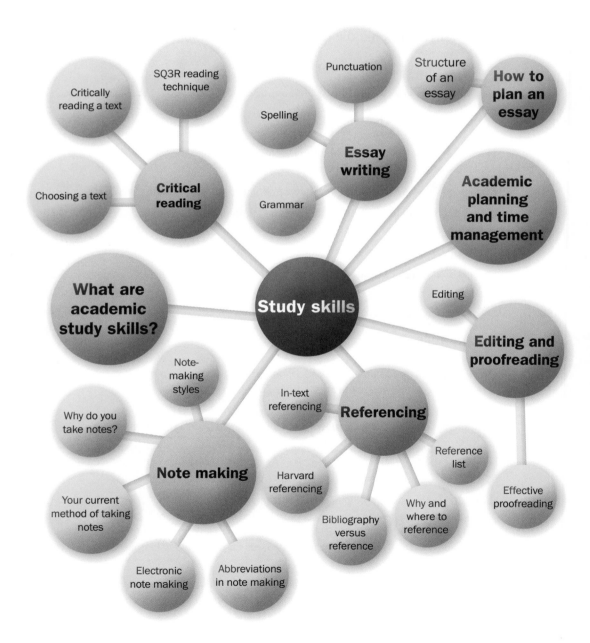

KEY WORDS

academic study skills, bibliography, critical reading, editing, grammar, linear notes, mnemonics, patterned notes, referencing, self-assessment, VARK questionnaire, word classes.

INTRODUCTION

It may be that you have not undertaken an academic qualification for a while, or you may never have completed an academic qualification outside of school. Whatever your circumstances, this chapter can provide you with a guide to navigating your qualification and getting the most from any reading and writing that you need to complete your units. In this way, this chapter aims to meet the following objectives:

o   to assist you in identifying any academic study skills areas you need to brush up on;

o   to support you in developing your academic writing skills;

o   to provide a scaffold for you to get the most from your academic reading.

WHAT ARE ACADEMIC STUDY SKILLS?

Good academic study skills will make your journey through any qualification much easier and ultimately more successful. Study skills encompass the ability to extract information from appropriate sources, take useful notes and write in an effective manner for a variety of audiences. The educational establishment where you are studying the level 4 CET qualification may have a website that has tools and resources to help with academic study skills; remember to use these sites. Many of these academic study skills can also be used with your own learners in one form or another. An effective starting point is to do a self-assessment of your skills; this will make it easier to navigate your way through this chapter.

STARTING POINT

Self-assessment audit

Use the self-assessment audit to rate your skills in the table below. Once you have completed it, follow the instructions at the end of the chart to help you navigate your way through this chapter.

Tick a box for how you feel about each skill.

1 = confident; 2 = need a brush-up; 3 = need support

Academic study skills	1	2	3	Sections in this chapter to find support
I am able to plan my time and meet deadlines				Academic planning and time management page 160
I know what learning styles work for me				Note making page 161
I can find information from different locations (books, journals and online resources)				Referencing page 175
I am able to reference sources of information				Referencing page 175
I can evaluate the information I find				Choosing a text page 165
I am able to employ reading techniques				Critical reading; SQ3R reading techniques page 166
I am able to critically analyse my academic reading				Critical reading; SQ3R reading techniques page 166
I can take useful notes from my reading				Note making page 161 Electronic note making page 164
I can take useful notes from listening to others				Note making page 161 Electronic note making page 164
I can effectively plan my writing for academic assignments				How to plan an essay page 167
I can write coherently and cohesively, in paragraphs				Editing and proofreading page 178
I am able to use grammar and punctuation correctly in assignments				Grammar; Spelling; Punctuation page 168
I am able to spell specialist words and employ spelling techniques				Mnemonics; Spelling page 171
I can proofread my work effectively				Effective proofreading page 178

Figure 10.1 Self-assessment audit

Once you have completed the audit then visit the pages where you have ticked *2* or *3* in the boxes; read through for a *brush-up* and read through and do the exercises for *need support*. Even if you have evaluated yourself as a *1* then it is still worthwhile to review this chapter, just to refresh yourself.

ACADEMIC PLANNING AND TIME MANAGEMENT

Many people taking the level 4 CET qualification will be doing so while working full or part time; this can create problems if time is not well planned. At the start of your qualification you should receive a calendar of key dates, which will give hand-in dates for assessments. Compare the qualification timetable with your own teaching and marking timetable and see if key dates overlap and if you are going to have times of the year where you are especially busy. Think about when a piece of work needs to be started in order to be able to hand it in on time.

A solution to this could be to use a time chart, like a Gantt chart. Henry Gantt (1910) developed the Gantt chart to illustrate start and finish dates of a project. Although it is possible to download free Gantt chart software, you can also create a Gantt chart in software spreadsheet programs such as Excel, or use Microsoft Visio or Project, if they are installed on your computer. There are lots of YouTube videos and tutorials on the internet that will tell you how to produce a Gantt chart in a spreadsheet program. Alternatively, a time chart can be written using old-fashioned pen and paper.

ID	Task Name	Start	Finish	Duration	Sep 2013		Oct 2013				Nov 2013				Dec 2013		
					22/9	29/9	6/10	13/10	20/10	27/10	3/11	10/11	17/11	24/11	1/12	8/12	15/12
1	Source set texts	27/09/2013	03/10/2013	1w													
2	Read and take notes	03/10/2013	16/10/2013	2w													
3	Plan assignment	16/10/2013	19/10/2013	.43w													
4	Write assignment	20/10/2013	02/11/2013	2w													
5	Edit	03/11/2013	06/11/2013	.43w													
6	Proofread	07/11/2013	13/11/2013	1w													
7	Submit assignment	15/11/2013	15/11/2013	.14w													
8	Write 4 reflective journals	10/10/2013	19/12/2013	10.14w													

Figure 10.2 Gantt chart created using Microsoft Visio

NOTE MAKING

Making effective notes is important to provide a method for recording and then recalling information. Active *note making* can also help you to understand the information you are reading or hearing. Active *note making* means thinking about what you are writing, looking for connections between pieces of information and using your own words. Passive *note taking* is about copying, underlining and not discriminating between what needs making note of and what does not.

Making notes that are still useful a few days after they have been made is a skill that can be developed. Firstly, you need to understand why you are taking the notes, then consider what you need to note and how you are going to lay out your notes.

Consider the following:

○ why you take notes;

○ your current method of taking notes;

○ alternative ways of taking notes.

Why do you take notes?

Note taking is an activity carried out by most learners, but what is the purpose of it? Before reading on, write down the reasons you have for taking notes. Then check whether they are similar to the suggestions that are provided below:

○ to provide a useful record of a writer's or speaker's key ideas;

○ to provide a useful record of where information has come from;

○ to help your memory;

○ to help with understanding, when reading;

○ to help you to make links between related ideas;

○ to help ideas flow;

○ to plan for a piece of writing;

○ to organise information;

○ to help exam revision.

Your current method of taking notes

Question

What method do you use for note making, or are you still at the note-taking stage?

Answer

Possible answers could include jotting down (or keying in) the main points that you think are important and want to recall at a later time.

Question

What notes have you taken in the past and why did you take them?

Answer

Possible answers could include study notes, notes to other people when you want to provide them with brief information or notes you make to yourself as a reminder to do something.

Reflect upon how useful these notes have been to you and what you could do differently to improve your note-making techniques (information relating to developing your skills of reflecting can be found in Chapter 1). Doing this should provide you with a strategy to change or enhance the way you take notes.

Note-making styles

Although there are many ways that you can make notes, they all stem from two basic types: linear and patterned forms. The way you find easiest will depend on you and your learning style, so it is good to try both and see which suits you.

According to Fleming's (2013) VARK (visual, auditory, read/write, kinaesthetic) guide to learning styles, linear notes are best for read/write learners who prefer their information displayed as words, while patterned notes are suitable for learners who like graphical or physical representations of information. To gather further information about your learning preferences, visit Fleming's website (see *Taking It Further* at the end of this chapter) to take a VARK questionnaire.

Linear notes

General advice (also good for patterned notes):

○ decide why you are taking the notes before you start;

○ be as brief as possible;

○ have a note-making system;

○ only use words you understand (look up any you do not understand);

○ leave lots of white space – you may want to add more notes at a later date.

Linear strategies:

○ don't write whole sentences;

○ use colour or arrows for underlining linked points;

○ abbreviations can be useful – see below;

○ pick out themes and link up points;

○ number points – could be in order of importance.

Avoid unhelpful strategies:

○ don't just copy – understand and write in own words;

○ don't waste time copying out notes to make them neater – if you can read them;

○ try to keep your handwriting legible.

Making notes more legible:

○ draw boxes around notes to make them stand out;

○ highlight floating bits of information;

○ colour-code key themes.

Patterned notes

Patterned notes can take many forms and go by different names, such as: mind-maps and spider-grams. They all have one thing in common: they all start in the middle and expand outwards.

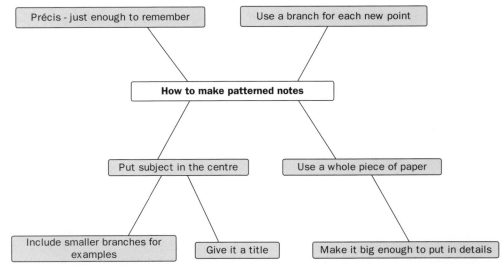

Figure 10.3 Mind-map created using free online software (Text2mindmap, 2013)

Abbreviations in note making

It is useful to use abbreviations as a shorthand method for taking notes efficiently. Be sure to always link the same abbreviation or symbol to the same word or meaning. You can create your own abbreviations or use standard abbreviations, like those in the activity at the end of this chapter.

Electronic note making

There are many applications (apps) available that can provide some form of electronic note making on devices such as tablets, note-books, laptops and desk-top computers. A simple online search will provide you with a list of apps suitable for all different kinds of note making. Be aware that some of the better apps may have to be purchased. Some devices come with proprietary software that is specifically designed for note taking and can be used with an external stylus. Whether you are using a pen and paper or a tablet and stylus, the same note-making tips and hints will apply.

CRITICAL READING

Critical reading is a very different activity from reading for pleasure. The ability to read critically, no matter how fluent a reader you are, is something that can be and needs to be developed. Critical reading enables you to read, understand and interrogate a text. This is not a passive activity and involves three main stages:

○   choosing a text;
○   critically reading the text;
○   using the information from the text.

Choosing a text

This may be as simple as looking at the reading lists provided at the end of each chapter in this book or in your CET award handbook, or you may need to find texts in your specialist teaching area. The educational organisation at which you are studying may have a library, and library staff are usually very helpful about how to find online and paper-based texts. Use their expertise; go on any library tours that are offered. Many organisations will have a good selection of online resources accessed through their own website, such as: articles, e-journals and e-books which are organised into subject areas.

Ask questions about any (non-set) texts that you are choosing.

Question

Does it need to be a current text?

Answer

Yes, it does need to be relatively recent – within the last few years, unless there is nothing more recent to use or you are going back to an original source of a theory, for example. Always check to see if you are using the most up-to-date edition of a book.

Question

How can you tell if a text is academically reliable?

Answer

If it is contained within an academic library then chances are it is worth reading. Look on the internet for reviews and also look at the publisher to see what else they have published.

Question

Are internet sites worth visiting?

Answer

Yes, but look at them in the same way as a book, ask questions and make a judgement to assess whether it is more anecdotal than academic.

Question

Wikipedia, yes or no?

Answer

There is nothing wrong with Wikipedia as a starting point for research or to get a simple definition but it should then lead you to other places from which to get your information.

Question

Are search engines, for example Google, the only way to go?

Answer

No, there are others that can be tried and used. The organisation that you are studying at may have links to various academic databases and search engines. You can also use websites such as Refseek (2013), which makes academic information accessible to all.

Critically reading a text

To be able to read and understand academic texts, you must engage in critical reading techniques. Critically reading a text is a way of making sure that you not only read and understand what is being read but you apply your critical reasoning to decide how much you believe what you have read, how you are going to use the information, and also if you need to read further.

SQ3R reading technique

SQ3R is a technique for reading effectively. The name of the technique comes from its five stages developed by Robinson (1946), which he called the Survey Q3R method of studying. There are other reading techniques for higher level reading, but they tend to follow similar paths. SQ3R can be used with your own learners either in its full form or in a scaled-down version. This reading technique is best undertaken when you can concentrate, so you need to remove yourself from other distractions.

The SQ3R stages

1. Survey: this stage is really about looking without reading. Look at the pictures, tables, headings and subheadings to start to understand the content of whatever you are reading.

2. Question: start to think about questions you could ask about the text you are reading. These could be specific to your subject or more general.

3. Read: read it actively. Think, as you read, about answers to the questions you have formulated, and think about why you are reading it.

4. Recite: think about what you have read. Is it helping with what you needed to know? Perhaps take notes to help with this stage or talk aloud.

5. Review: challenge yourself to see if you can remember what you have written. Identify key words and ideas and see if you understand them without relying on the text.

HOW TO PLAN AN ESSAY

At this level of academic writing, you must plan your writing to ensure that you include everything that you need to. You can write an essay without planning, but you can write a much better essay with planning. Firstly, you must read the assignment brief to understand what you need to do. If you do not understand it, talk to a tutor and make sure you understand the remit of the assignment. This is one of the most important stages: it is amazing how many people do not read an assignment brief before embarking on an assignment and can end up failing because of this. Once you have done the reading needed, you can begin work on planning your essay (if that is what is needed).

Question

What benefits do you get from planning an essay?

Answer

The benefits you get are:

o a coherent argument;

o a logical structure;

o you do not have to juggle all of your ideas in your head;

o you answer the question(s) asked of you.

Everyone is different, so you need to decide which way is best for you, but you need to plan three steps:

o take notes from your reading;

o extract the ideas from your reading and get ideas down on paper;

o arrange these ideas into the structure of the essay.

You can plan any of these steps using a note-making technique – linear or patterned notes or a mixture. Be prepared to have to update your plans as you start to write your essay.

Structure of an essay

Introduction – tell your audience what question you will be answering or what you will be addressing; say how you will go about it and define any specialist terms, if necessary. It can be easier to write the introduction once you have finished the rest of the assignment.

Main body – there should be one main point in each paragraph, each paragraph should address the question; group ideas and themes together. A good way is to think of each paragraph as if it were a mini essay on its own. So open with an introductory sentence outlining what the paragraph is going to be about and finish with a sentence that concludes the paragraph by saying what is in the paragraph.

Conclusion – summarise what you have written, come to a conclusion, if necessary, and show how it answers the question; never add any new evidence in the conclusion. Your introduction and conclusion, together, should give a reader a road map of the rest of your essay.

ESSAY WRITING

Academic writing style is very different from everyday writing and you need to employ different techniques within:

- ○   grammar;
- ○   spelling;
- ○   punctuation.

Grammar

This is not meant to be a definitive guide to grammar, it is meant to be a guide to the common problems encountered when writing an academic essay. If English is not your first language then you may be able to get extra help and support – ask your tutor.

Question

What do we mean by grammar?

Answer

Grammar is the structural foundation of our ability to express ourselves. The more we are aware of how it works, the more we can monitor the meaning and effectiveness of the way we and others use language. It can help foster precision, detect ambiguity, and exploit the richness of expression available in English. And it can help everyone – not only teachers of English, but teachers of anything, for all teaching is ultimately a matter of getting to grips with meaning. (Crystal, 2004, p 20)

In academic writing, grammar becomes quite prescriptive and it is good to have a foundation of grammar to help you check your written work. This can also help you to analyse and diagnose grammatical issues your learners have with written English. With this in mind, it is useful to have an understanding of the main word classes; this not only helps you to understand how a sentence is constructed, it also helps when reading grammatical self-help books and websites.

Problems with nouns

Knowing when to put a capital on a noun can be problematic. Common nouns do not need a capital letter and proper nouns do. Proper nouns are the individual names of things, places or people; common nouns are the names of general items.

Example

I kicked the ball *and broke the window where the* May Ball *was being held.*

The main thing to watch out for is inconsistency: if you capitalise a noun then do so throughout a piece of work.

Problems with pronouns

A pronoun can replace a noun in a sentence to avoid repetition.

Example

Maslow's hierarchy of needs was part of a theory he proposed in 1943.

Instead of repeating the name again, we can replace it with a pronoun (he, she, it, they). However, problems can arise when the reader does not know who or what the pronoun is referring to.

Example

Maslow researched Albert Einstein. He believed in examining the positive qualities in people.

In this case, the reader is not sure if Maslow or Einstein believed in examining the positive qualities in people. When misunderstanding can occur, it is better to not use a pronoun:

Maslow researched Albert Einstein. Maslow believed in examining the positive qualities in people. Or it could be rewritten to avoid using Maslow's name twice: *Maslow, who believed in examining the positive qualities in people, researched Einstein.*

Problems with verbs

Problems can arise in choosing whether to use the passive voice or active voice.

○   The active voice is when the subject of the sentence performs the action: *I researched all of the books on Skinner.*

○   The passive voice is when the action is done to the subject: *All of the books on Skinner were researched.*

Academic writing tends to use the passive voice because it makes the writing appear more objective and it helps with eliminating 'I' from the writing. Academic writing avoids using 'I' except where you are asked to use it in cases such as reflective writing outlined in Chapter 1. Overuse of the passive voice can make writing unnecessarily complicated, however. If use of the passive voice avoids using 'I' then go with it. If it merely makes a sentence sound overly complicated, then avoid using it. Passive voice is the normal voice to use when writing up experiments.

Problems with adjectives and adverbs

At school we are often encouraged to use adjectives and adverbs to make our writing more interesting. An adjective describes a noun and an adverb describes how the action of a verb is performed. When using adjectives and adverbs for academic purposes, make sure that they make the writing more precise, not more interesting. You should also avoid superlatives (a superlative is the highest degree of something: best, biggest, greatest, most complicated), unless you know for sure that it is the best, biggest, etc.

Problems with sentences

At an academic level, you are not expected merely to write in simple sentences, you need to put ideas together and therefore show the relationship between them. Every sentence contains at least one main clause. A main clause can stand on its own or as part of a complex or compound sentences. A subordinate clause cannot stand on its own and exists as part of a complex sentence.

> ## *Examples*
>
> Assessment informs progress – main clause
>
> Assessment recognises achievement – main clause
>
> Assessment informs progress and recognises achievement – compound sentence made from combining two main clauses by adding a conjunction (and, but, so, etc.)
>
> The learners will become plumbers – main clause
>
> After they have achieved their qualifications – subordinate clause
>
> After they have achieved their qualifications, they will become plumbers – complex sentence created by combining a main clause and a subordinate clause

A problem that often occurs in academic writing is when using a relative clause. A relative clause is a subordinate clause connected to a main clause using a relative pronoun: *that, whom, which, whose, when, who* or *where*. People get confused about which connecting word to use, and this is made more confusing by the fact that often there is more than one right way to connect these kinds of sentences.

○ He was the only person **who** made sure the assessment was fair.

○ He was the only person that made sure the assessment was fair.

○ It is a qualification **that** should be taken by everyone.

○ It is a qualification **which** should be taken by everyone.

The situation in which *that* would not be a suitable connecting word is when using relative clauses. There are two kinds of relative clauses, defining and non-defining. A non-defining relative clause adds extra information, while a defining relative clause adds information vital to the previous clause. A non-defining relative clause never uses *that* and always has comma/s to separate it from the rest of the sentence.

Defining and non-defining relative clauses

It reminded her of the qualification that/which she took at university.

This is a defining relative clause because you need the clause about university to know which qualification it reminded her of and it is not separated by a comma.

My French teacher, who is actually from France, is giving us a test next week.

This is a non-defining relative clause because the fact that the teacher is French is not essential to the sentence and it is closed off from the rest of the sentence by commas.

Spelling

You do not need to be able to spell perfectly, but you do need to know your own spelling weaknesses so that you are able to employ strategies to help you and your learners to be able to spell effectively. One strategy is, of course, the spellchecker on your computer. However, computerised spellcheckers have their limitations, so do not rely on them, and use your dictionary.

Mnemonics

If you regularly struggle with a word then a memory trick is one way to fix the spelling in your mind. This can also help when you are writing on a whiteboard in the classroom.

Examples

- o   a *piece* of *pie*;
- o   *add* an *address*;
- o   big elephants can't *always* *use* small exits (because);
- o   *necessary* has one collar and two socks.

Problem spellings

There are a number of common words that are often confused, so pay particular attention to these.

Examples

Their, they're and there

Their is possessive, so it needs to own something.

Their theories are worth considering.

They're is a shortening of *they are.*

They're going to try an active learning approach. (Don't use contractions in academic writing.)

There refers to an idea or a place.

Don't go in there.

Your and you're

Your is possessive, you own something.

Your classroom needs to be tidied.

You're is a shortening of *you are.*

You're going to clean the classroom. (No contractions.)

It's and its

It's is a shortening of *it is* or *it has.*

It's your assessment strategy. (No contractions)

Its is possessive, it owns something.

Its cover had been written all over.

Definitely

There is definitely no 'a' in *definitely*, contrary to popular belief.

Table 10.1 Some commonly confused words

Word 1	Meaning	Word 2	Meaning
accept	to agree; to receive; do	except	not including
advice	recommendation about what to do	advise	to recommend something
affect	to change or make a difference to	effect	a result; to bring about a result
all together	all in one place; all at once	altogether	completely; on the whole
aloud	out loud	allowed	permitted
assent	agreement, approval	ascent	the action of rising or climbing up
censure	to criticise strongly	censor	to ban parts of a book or film; a person who does this
complement	to add to so as to improve	compliment	to praise or express approval
council	a group of people who manage or advise	counsel	advice; to advise
currant	a dried grape	current	happening now; a flow of water, air, or electricity
defuse	to make a situation less tense	diffuse	to spread over a wide area
discreet	careful not to attract attention	discrete	separate and distinct
draught	a current of air	draft	first version of a piece of writing
elicit	to draw out a reply or reaction	illicit	not allowed by law or rules
ensure	to make certain that something will happen	insure	to provide compensation if a person dies or property is damaged
foreword	an introduction to a book	forward	onwards; ahead
imply	to suggest indirectly	infer	to draw a conclusion
loose	to unfasten; to set free	lose	to be deprived of; to be unable to find
militate	to be a powerful factor against	mitigate	to make less severe
practice	the use of an idea or method; the work or business of a doctor, etc.	practise	to do something repeatedly to gain skill; to do something regularly
prescribe	to authorise use of medicine; to order authoritatively	proscribe	to officially forbid something
principal	most important; the head of a school	principle	a fundamental rule or belief
sight	the ability to see	site	a location

Source: Oxforddictionaries.com, 2013

Punctuation

The colon and semicolon

In academic writing, it is expected that you will use the colon and semicolon, as appropriate. Use sparingly, and if you are not sure – omit.

A colon has two dots, one above the other (:), while a semicolon consists of a comma with a dot above it (;).

> ## *Examples*
>
> ### The colon
>
> The colon is often used to introduce a list of items.
>
> *You will need to bring three things to the classroom: a pen, a piece of paper and a computer.*
>
> A colon can also be used to introduce an explanation or a definition of something.
>
> *I'll tell you what I'm going to do: I'm going to quit smoking!*
>
> *Mouse (noun): a small mammal belonging to the order of rodents.*
>
> ### The semicolon
>
> The semicolon is often employed to join two independent clauses, ie it joins two clauses that could be sentences.
>
> *Mary teaches ICT; Joanne teaches business studies.*
>
> These two clauses could be separate sentences. However, when we use a semicolon, we are usually suggesting that there is a relationship between the sentences, but we are not making that relationship clear. Usually, you can tell from the context what the relationship is.
>
> One more very common use of the semicolon is to join two clauses using a transition such as *however, therefore,* or *on the other hand.*
>
> *She works all day; in addition, she teaches Literacy in the evenings.*
>
> *You should get your computer fixed; otherwise, you might lose your work.*

Apostrophes

Apostrophes are punctuation marks used to show possession and omission. The simple rule in academic writing is that you do not use contractions, always write the word out in full: Don't = do not

Apostrophes of possession are commonly misused in assignments. Here are some simple rules to follow.

Examples

Rules for apostrophes of possession

To show singular possession add an apostrophe plus 's' to the noun:

The boy's pen

The man's homework

Add an extra 's' to names ending in an 's' or an 's' or 'z' sound:

Mr Jones's classroom

Use an apostrophe where the implied noun should be:

That was his friend's, not his, homework.

To use the apostrophe with a plural, make the noun plural then use the apostrophe:

The girls' bags

When capital letters and numbers are pluralised and used as nouns, do not use an apostrophe:

CDs were invented in the 1980s.

REFERENCING

Why and where to reference

As part of your academic writing, you are going to read works by other people and will want to use their theories and ideas to support your own. In academic writing, you must reference your work so that you are giving credit to the person who has done the hard work. Careful referencing means you cannot be accused of plagiarism and it shows you have researched your work and it has academic veracity. Otherwise your work can look as if it is merely anecdotal with no research to support it. The educational establishment at which you are studying will tell you what method of referencing they want you to use and you must follow what they say. One of the most common forms of referencing at the moment is Harvard referencing, though other forms are used (eg footnotes).

Bibliography versus reference list

At this level you are probably not going to be asked to provide a bibliography, just a reference list. However, it is still good to know what the difference is. A bibliography is where you list all of the books, journals, websites and other sources that you have read, but which you may not have referred to in your assignment, as well as those that you have actually used. A reference list is where you provide details of just the books, journals, websites, etc. that you have actually referred to in your assignment.

Harvard referencing

There are two places in an assignment where you need to complete your referencing.

○ In the main body of your assignment – called in-text referencing or citing – you will refer to theories and ideas to support your writing. With in-text referencing, generally you should only include the author's surname (no initials) and the date, and possibly a page number.

○ All the sources you cite in the text must be included in the References, usually at the end of the assignment. This is where you list alphabetically all of the references that you have used in your assignment so that the reader can easily locate the sources of your citations. You must refer to the author in exactly the same way as you referred to them in your text.

In-text referencing

Citations

Citations are where you have read someone else's work, and then you have put it into your own words. Citations are better than direct quotations because it shows to your tutor that you have thought about and understood what you have read.

Example

Maslow (1943) proposed that as humans, we are driven by certain needs. A pyramid structure is frequently used to represent these needs, with the most basic needs being represented at the bottom.

You must include a reference every time you refer to any source that includes government Acts or legislation. A date alone is not enough: you need to include the sources as well as the date.

Example

The Tomlinson Report (FEFC, 1996), was a key contributor to the development of inclusive practice in the Further Education and Skills sector.

Direct quotes

Try to use any direct quotes sparingly. If you do use them, they should be placed in quotation marks, with the author's name, date and page number.

Example

The Tomlinson Report (FEFC, 1996, p12) suggested the 'redesign of the very process of learning, assessment and organisation so as to fit the objectives and learning styles of the learners'.

Quotes that are more than two lines of text should be separated from the main text and indented, followed by the reference and page number.

Example

The report emphasised:

'That learners with learning difficulties or disabilities should be considered first and foremost as learners suggesting the redesign [of] the very *process of learning, assessment and organisation so as to fit the objectives and learning styles of the learners.*'

(FEFC, 1996, p12)

Secondary referencing

Secondary referencing occurs when you are reading a book or journal article whose author uses facts or information from research done by someone else, and you want to use this to support your own assignment. Try to avoid secondary referencing as much as possible by going back to the original source. If that is not possible, here is an example of how to reference a secondary source:

Maslow (1943), as cited in Hillier (2007)

The reference list at the end of the text only needs to give the details of the source/s that you have actually read. In this case, you would simply refer to the main text (Hillier, 2007) as follows:

Hillier, Y. (2007), *Reflective Teaching in Further and Adult Education*, 2nd edn. London: Continuum International.

Internet referencing

You may reference from the internet, but the rule is 'if you cannot find an author, try not to use it'. In this sense, an author does not have to be a named person or persons; it could be an organisation or a national body. There is a lot of unreliable material on the internet. Wikipedia should be regarded as a research starting point, not the end point. For in-text citation of an internet source, simply cite the author/organisation and date, never put the website address.

Example

The Leitch Review of Skills (HMSO, 2006) was an attempt to undertake an independent review of the UK's long-term skills needs.

Reference list

A complete list of all the sources you have included within the main body of your assignment must be provided at the end of the assignment, under the heading 'Reference List'. Double check to ensure there are no references in your text that are not included in your list, and nothing in your list that is not in your text. A reference list is a vital part of your assignment and is not an 'add-on extra'. Take time to prepare it – it will always take longer than you think. References must be listed in alphabetical order by surname or organisation. You do not need to separate the reference list into categories or sections, for example: books, legislation and websites, unless you are asked to do so. Remember that you do not need to provide a separate 'Bibliography' of material that you have read but not used (unless it is specifically asked for).

Example

Ghaye, T. (2011) *Teaching and Learning Through Reflective Practice: A Practical Guide for Positive Action*. Oxon: Routledge.

Hatton, N., and Smith, D. (2005) Reflection in teacher education – towards definition and implementation. *Teaching and Teacher Education*, 11(1): 33–39.

Hillier, Y. (2005) *Reflective Teaching in Further and Adult Education*, 2nd edn. London: Continuum International.

EDITING AND PROOFREADING

So, once you have completed your assignment, your last task is still very important. At this level of academic writing, it is not enough to just write something, proofread it then hand the assignment in. You must edit and proofread. This stage could effectively mean rewriting some of your work, so you need to leave plenty of time.

Editing

When editing work you need to be ready to make significant changes to the text, if needed. Editing is carried out when the first draft is completed. Do not try editing until that first draft is completed because constantly stopping and starting will make the writing process much longer and will interfere with the flow of writing.

The first step in the editing process is to go back to the assessment criteria and make sure that the assignment covers the criteria. Check the word count, the assessment criteria and any criteria for grading, such as a pass, merit or distinction. Then remove any sections that are not pertinent to the assignment or take it over the word count. Most academic writing allows you to be 10 per cent under or over the word count, but please check; do not assume this is the case.

The second step is to check any conventions laid down by the educational organisation. There might be a specified font type and size, you may need to double space the lines or print only on one side of the paper. If no guidelines have been mentioned, set your own and stick to them throughout the work. Typical conventions for academic writing include:

o   font size of 12;

o   non-serif font, or a transitional serif such as Times New Roman;

o   1.5 or double line spacing;

o   left justified paragraphs;

o   insert page numbers and your name, or student number, on each page.

The third step is to check that the piece of work makes sense. Do paragraphs logically follow each other? Is the writing clear and easy to understand? If there is an argument, has it been proved with credible sources of evidence?

The last step is to make sure that all sources of evidence are referenced and that those sources are credible. This is vital to ensure you are not plagiarising anyone's work and that your statements are not just anecdotal but can be verified.

Effective proofreading

I was working on the proof of one of my poems all the morning, and took out a comma. In the afternoon I put it back again. Credited to Oscar Wilde (Sherard, 1902, p72)

These proofreading steps do not have to be done in this order and some steps may be left out, depending on the kind of writing being proofread:

o   leave the assignment and come back to it fresh. This can help with reading the text that has been written, rather than just reading what you think you have written;

o   print out a copy to proofread. Most people will see errors on paper that they do not see on the screen;

o   choose one type of error to proofread for at a time – and stick to it: spellings, then punctuation and so on;

o   read the text aloud. This can be a good way to identify mistakes – when you stumble over a sentence it is usually because of the way it has been written;

o   use the spellchecker but do not rely on it; also use a dictionary for homophones (see list of commonly confused words);

o   check facts and figures, and make sure that evidence is referenced and from a credible source (see above for how to reference work);

o   reflect on the kinds of mistakes you have made in the past and check for those. If you have had feedback from a previous assignment then review that feedback and check your current assignment for those errors.

SUMMARY

Whether, for example, you are preparing resources for teaching, completing paperwork or writing assignments it is important that you produce work that is accurate and well presented. The intention of this chapter is to support you in achieving this.

 Check your understanding

You will find suggested answers to some of these questions at the back of this book.

Activity 1: Create your own time chart to cover either the duration of your qualification or an assignment. Remember to build in other factors such as when you may be very busy at work or away on holiday, which means you will need to start an assignment sooner. As well as assignments, include observations, any peer or experienced practitioner observations you need to do and your reflective journal. The key is to try to keep to your time chart as much as possible and update it so it does not become worthless.

Activity 2: See how many abbreviations you recognise, then check your answers at the end of the book. Use the last few blank lines to add some of your own abbreviations to use when taking notes.

Abbreviation/symbol	Meaning
eg	for example
=	
etc.	
≠	
cf.	
∴	
et al.	
∵	
ibid.	
\+	
N.B. or n.b.	
-	
viz	
>	
<	
≫	

Abbreviation/symbol	Meaning
«	
≥	
%	
÷	
x	
^	
→	
↑	
↓	
ie	
&	
P or p	
sp	
// or para	
C20	

(Staffordshire University, 2011)

Activity 3:   Fill in the definition of the main word classes and provide examples.

Class	Definition	Example highlighted in a sentence
Nouns		
Pronouns		
Verbs		
Adjectives		
Adverbs		
Prepositions		
Conjunctions		

Activity 4:   In each of the sentences below cross out which commonly confused word is not needed.

1.   The principle/principal matter is that no one is hurt.

2.   I did not mean to imply/infer that the learner was lying.

3.   They all agreed to complete the homework, accept/except for James.

4.   The affect/effect of the experiment was total destruction.

5.   I gave my ascent/assent to the field trip.

6. He tried to defuse/diffuse the situation by laughing.

7. I will not lose/loose my homework.

8. The main building site/sight was in a total mess.

9. I need to practise/practice my handwriting.

10. She tried to elicit/illicit an answer from the quietest learner.

Activity 5: Put defining (D) or non-defining (N-D) next to these sentences.

Sentence with relative clause	D or N-D
This is the assignment that I wrote when I was at university.	
Maslow, whose first name is Abraham, developed the hierarchy of needs theory in 1943.	
This is the behaviourist theory which Skinner innovated.	
Active learning, which puts the responsibility of learning on learners, was popularised by Bonwell and Eison.	
The assignment which I wrote is very short.	

Activity 6: For your next assignment, go through all of the steps for the editing and proofreading before handing in your assignment. Save all drafts of your assignment and compare your first draft with the finished draft that you are handing in.

Activity 7: Write the correct referencing for the following kinds of texts. You will need to do some research on Harvard Referencing sites to be able to correctly reference the different types of text (see *Taking It Further* at the end of this chapter).

○ a journal article;

○ a book;

○ an edited book;

○ a chapter from an edited book;

○ a page on a website;

○ a government report.

Activity 8: Next time you need to take notes, try a different way of note making and see if it makes a difference to the quality of your notes.

End of chapter reflections: Outline five key points that you have learned from reading this chapter.

 TAKING IT FURTHER

In addition to the literature already commented upon in this chapter you may find the following literature of interest.

Harvard Referencing System – guide and examples: www.staffs.ac.uk/support_depts/infoservices/learning_support/refzone/harvard/index.jsp [accessed January 2015].

Levin, P. (2007) *Skilful Time Management, Student Friendly Guides*. Buckingham: Open University Press.

McMillan, K., and Weyers, J. (2007) *How to Write Essays and Assignments*. Harlow: Pearson Education.

Price, G., and Maier, P. (2007) *Effective Study Skills: Unlock Your Potential*. Essex: Pearson.

The Open University (2007) *Time Management Tips*. Buckingham: Open University Press.

VARK – A Guide to Learning Styles, www.vark-learn.com/english/index.asp [accessed January 2015].

REFERENCES

Crystal, D. (2004) *In Word and Deed*. [online]. Available at: www.tes.co.uk/article.aspx?storycode=393984 [accessed January 2015].

ETF (2014) *Professional Standards for Teachers and Trainers in Education and Training*. [online]. Available at: www.et-foundation.co.uk [accessed May 2014].

Fleming, N. (2013) *VARK – A Guide to Learning Styles*. [online]. Available at: www.vark-learn.com/english/index.asp [accessed January 2015].

Gantt, H. (1910) *Work, Wages and Profit*. New York: The Engineering Magazine Company.

Oxforddictionaries.com (2013) *Commonly Confused Words*. [online]. Available at: www.oxforddictionaries.com/words/commonly-confused-words [accessed January 2015].

Refseek (2013) *Refseek*. [online]. Available at: www.refseek.com [accessed January 2015].

Robinson, F. (1946) *Effective Study*. New York: Harper and Row.

Sherard, R. (1902) *Oscar Wilde: The Story and an Unhappy Friendship, with Portrait and Facsimile Letters*. London: Hermes Press.

Staffordshire University (2011) *Note Taking*. [online]. http://www.staffs.ac.uk/askv1/steps/notes.php [accessed August 2015].

Text2mindmap (2013) *Mindmaps*. [online]. Available from:www.text2mindmap.com [accessed January 2015].

Glossary of acronyms

ADHD	Attention Deficit Hyperactivity Disorder
AO	Awarding Organisation
APL	Accreditation of Prior Learning
ASCL	Association of School and College Leaders
ATL	Association of Teachers and Lecturers
ATLS	Associate Teacher Lecturing and Skills
BDA	British Dyslexia Association
BIS	Department for Business, Innovation and Skills
CAVTL	Commission on Adult Vocational Teaching and Learning
CET	Certificate in Education and Training
CIF	Common Inspection Framework
COSHH	Control of Substances Hazardous to Health
CPD	Continuing Professional Development
CRB	Criminal Records Bureau
CTLLS	Certificate in Teaching in the Lifelong Learning Sector
DBS	Disclosure and Barring Service
DET	Diploma in Education and Training
DfES	Department for Education and Skills
DIUS	Department for Industry, University and Skills
DTLLS	Diploma in Teaching in the Lifelong Learning Sector
EFA	Education Funding Agency
EHRC	Equality and Human Rights Commission
EQF	European Qualification Framework
ESOL	English for Speakers of Other Languages
ETF	Education and Training Foundation
FE	Further Education
FEDA	Further Education Development Agency
FEFC	Further Education Funding Council
FENTO	Further Education National Training Organisation
Fog	Index Calculation that gives a numerical value equivalent to the number of years of education a person would need in order to be able to understand a text
GCSE	General Certificate of Secondary Education
HE	Higher education
HEI	Higher education institute
HSE	Health and Safety Executive
ICT	Information and Communication Technology
IfL	Institute for Learning
ILP	Individual learning plan
ISA	Independent Safeguarding Authority
ITE	Initial Teacher Education
ITT	Initial Teacher Training
LLS	Lifelong learning sector

LLUK	Lifelong Learning UK
LRC	Learning resource centre
LSA	Learning Support Assistant
LSC	Learning and Skills Council
LSIS	Learning Skills Improvement Services
NARIC	National Recognition Information Centre
NIACE	National Institute of Adult and Continuing Education
NQF	National Qualifications Framework
Ofqual	Office of Qualifications and Examinations Regulation
Ofsted	Office for Standards in Education
PCET	Post-compulsory Education and Training
PGCE	Postgraduate Certificate in Education
PISA	Programme for International Student Assessment
PTLLS	Preparing to Teach in the Lifelong Learning Sector
QCF	Qualifications and Credit Framework
QTLS	Qualified Teacher Learning and Skills
RARPA	Recognising and Recording Progress and Achievement
RPL	Recognition of Prior Learning
SEN	Special Educational Needs
SFA	Skills Funding Agency
SMART	Specific, measurable, attainable, relevant, time bound
SQ3R	Survey, question, read, recite, review
SWOT	Strengths, weaknesses, opportunities and threats
TA	Transactional analysis
TALENT	Training adult literacy, ESOL and numeracy teachers
UCU	University and College Union
VARK	Visual, auditory, read/write, kinaesthetic

Appendix 1: Chapter links to the ETF Professional Standards

STANDARD	CHAPTER
Professional values and attributes	
Develop your own judgement of what works and does not work in your teaching and training	
1 Reflect on what works best in your teaching and learning to meet the diverse needs of learners	Chapter 1
	Chapter 8
	Chapter 9
2 Evaluate and challenge your practice, values and beliefs	Chapter 1
	Chapter 8
3 Inspire, motivate and raise aspirations of learners through your enthusiasm and knowledge	Chapter 8
4 Be creative and innovative in selecting and adapting strategies to help learners to learn	Chapter 8
5 Value and promote social and cultural diversity, equality of opportunity and inclusion	Chapter 3
	Chapter 4
	Chapter 8
6 Build positive and collaborative relationships with colleagues and learners	Chapter 2
Professional knowledge and understanding	
Develop deep and critically informed knowledge and understanding in theory and practice	
7 Maintain and update knowledge of your subject and/or vocational area	Chapter 2
	Chapter 9
8 Maintain and update your knowledge of educational research to develop evidence- based practice	Chapter 8
	Chapter 9
9 Apply theoretical understanding of effective practice in teaching, learning and assessment drawing on research and other evidence	Chapter 3
	Chapter 4
	Chapter 8
	Chapter 9
10 Evaluate your practice with others and assess its impact on learning	Chapter 1
	Chapter 8
	Chapter 9
11 Manage and promote positive learner behaviour	Chapter 2
	Chapter 8
12 Understand the teaching and professional role and your responsibilities	Chapter 2
	Chapter 8

Professional skills	
Develop your expertise and skills to ensure the best outcomes for learners	
13 Motivate and inspire learners to promote achievement and develop their skills to enable progression	Chapter 4
	Chapter 8
14 Plan and deliver effective learning programmes for diverse groups or individuals in a safe and inclusive environment	Chapter 2
	Chapter 8
15 Promote the benefits of technology and support learners in its use	Chapter 8
16 Address the mathematics and English needs of learners and work creatively to overcome individual barriers to learning	Chapter 8
17 Enable learners to share responsibility for their own learning and assessment, setting goals that stretch and challenge	Chapter 3
	Chapter 4
	Chapter 8
18 Apply appropriate and fair methods of assessment and provide constructive and timely feedback to support progression and achievement	Chapter 3
	Chapter 4
	Chapter 8
19 Maintain and update your teaching and training expertise and vocational skills through collaboration with employers	Chapter 2
	Chapter 9
20 Contribute to organisational development and quality improvement through collaboration with others	Chapter 9

Education and Training Foundation (May 2014)

Appendix 2: Optional units available for the level 4 CET qualification

The table below lists a number of optional units that are available at levels 3, 4 and 5. In order for you to achieve the level 4 CET qualification you need to achieve 15 credits from this group. Other optional units are also available for you from the awards relating to Mathematics for Numeracy Teaching and English for Literacy and Language Teaching. You will find the list for these, as well as any new optional units that have been added, on the LSIS website: www.excellencegateway.org.uk/node/65. Furthermore, your tutor should be able to provide you with advice about what optional units are available to you.

Optional units for the level 4 CET qualification

Unit title	Level	Credit value
Action learning to support specific development of subject specific pedagogy	5	15
Action research	5	15
Assess occupational competence in the work environment (Learning and Development unit)	3	6
Assess vocational skills, knowledge and understanding (Learning and Development unit)	3	6
Assessment and support for the recognition of prior learning through the accreditation of learning outcomes	3	6
Delivering employability skills	4	6
Develop and prepare resources for learning and development (Learning and Development unit)	4	6
Develop learning and development programmes. (Learning and Development unit)	4	6
Developing, using and organising resources within a specialist area	5	15
Effective partnership working in the teaching and learning context	4	15
Engage learners in the learning and development process (Learning and Development unit)	3	6
Engage with employers to develop and support learning provision	3	6
Engage with employers to facilitate workforce development (Learning and Development unit)	4	6
Equality and diversity	4	6
Evaluating learning programmes	4	3
Identify individual learning and development needs (Learning and Development unit)	3	3
Identify the learning needs of organisations (Learning and Development unit)	4	6

Unit title	Level	Credit value
Internally assure the quality of assessment organisations (Learning and Development unit)	4	6
Manage learning and development in groups *(Learning and Development unit)*	4	6
Preparing for the coaching role	4	3
Preparing for the mentoring role	4	3
Preparing for the personal tutoring role	4	3
Principles and practice of lip-reading teaching	4	12
Specialist delivery techniques and activities	4	9
Teaching in a specialist area	4	15
Understanding and managing behaviours in a learning environment	5	15
Understanding the principles and practices of externally assuring the quality of assessment organisations (Learning and Development unit)	4	6
Understanding the principles and practices of internally assuring the quality of assessment organisations (Learning and Development unit)	4	6
Working with the 14–19 age range in the learning environment	4	9

Source: LSIS (May, 2013) qualifications Guidance For Awarding Organisations: Level Four Certificate In Education And Training (QCF)

 TAKING IT FURTHER

Excellence Gateway: addressing literacy, language, numeracy and ICT needs in education and training; defining the minimum core of teachers' knowledge, understanding and personal skills: www.excellencegateway.org.uk/node/12019

LSIS (2013) Qualifications Guidance for awarding organisations: Level Five Certificate in Education and Training including level five specialist pathway (QCF): www.excellencegateway.org.uk/node/65

Machin, L., Hindmarch, D., Richardson, T., Murray, S., (2014) *A Complete Guide to the Level 5 Diploma in Education and Training*, Northwich, Critical Publishing.

REFERENCES

LSIS (2013) Qualifications Guidance for Awarding Organisations: Level Four Certificate in Education and Training (QCF): www.excellencegateway.org.uk/node/65

LSIS (2013) Qualifications Guidance for awarding organisations: Optional units for QCF Education and Training qualifications (QCF): www.excellencegateway.org.uk/node/65

Appendix 3: Scheme of work template

Scheme of work

Teacher:		Course title:		Awarding body:		

Course aims:

Level:

Course length:

Lesson length:

Day(s):

Time:

Week	Learning outcomes	Teaching / learning methods	Assessment methods	Resources			

Appendix 4: Teaching and learning plan template

Teaching and learning plan

Teacher:	Course title:	Awarding body:
Location:	Date:	Time:
Number of learners:	Resources:	

Lesson aims:

Objectives – by the end of the lesson:

- all learners must...

- some learners will...

- a few learners may...

Equality and diversity/inclusivity:

Development of Functional Skills:

Time	Teacher activity	Learner activity	Assessment	Resources

Appendix 5: CPD reflective template

(for Activity 1, Chapter 9)

Continuous Professional Development
Name: Date:
Name of training event:
Brief details (date, length of course, who delivered it, internal or external):
Participants:
Were other people from your workplace on the course?
Key learning outcomes:*
What did you learn/discover? (brief notes):
Reflections:
How can this be used in your teaching and learning?
Action points:
What actions do you need to take to use what you have learned in your job (do you need further training on this, do you need to speak to a line manager, can what you have learned be cascaded to other members of staff)?

*If you did not learn/discover anything useful, please use the boxes above to explain why this was (perhaps the training was not at the right level for you or it was not appropriate for your job) and outline what training would be more suitable for you to discuss with your line manager.

Answers to activities

CHAPTER 1

Activity 1 Answers could include:

- to look back on an event and think about how well it went and what, if anything, could be done differently;
- to take stock of a situation in order to learn from it;
- to consider an event and/or action from various viewpoints in order to change and be able to improve our own development;
- to analyse a critical incident in order to act differently next time;
- to look critically at our actions and plan for change.

Activity 2 Answers could include:

- assists in providing an explanation for your experiences;
- helps to inform your future actions and strategies;
- can transform your thinking;
- questions your attitudes, beliefs, assumptions;
- puts actions, events and experiences into perspective;
- can be instrumental in any intervention and change processes.

Activity 3 Answers could include:

- describes and analyses events and incidents;
- involves the use of meta-cognition;
- challenges assumptions, biases and beliefs;
- questioning why you do things as you do;
- seeks out the opinions of others in order to inform your actions.

Activity 10 Answers could include:

- paragraph two is a descriptive writing account of how the author planned and observed the teaching and learning lesson;
- paragraph three draws paragraph two out a little more through descriptive reflection;
- paragraphs four, five, seven and eight are also descriptive;

- paragraphs six and ten provide dialogic reflective accounts;
- paragraph eleven draws the conclusion through critical reflection.

End of chapter reflections   Answers could include:

- knowing why, how and when to reflect;
- understanding what to reflect upon;
- understanding and also being able to apply theoretical models of reflection to your practice. For example, Schön's in-action and on-action model;
- knowing that there are different levels of reflection;
- how important reflection is to the development of your practice.

CHAPTER 2

Activity 2   Relating to EHRC guidance (2015) answers could include:

- *Direct discrimination* occurs when you treat a student less favourably than you treat (or would treat) another student because of a protected characteristic. So a very basic example would be refusing to admit a student because of their race, for example, because they are Roma. It is not possible to justify direct discrimination, so it is always unlawful. There are, however, exceptions to the further and higher education provisions that allow, for example, single-sex institutions to admit only students of one gender without this being unlawful direct discrimination;

- *Indirect discrimination* occurs when you apply a provision, criteria or practice in the same way for all students or a particular student group, such as postgraduate students, but this has the effect of putting students sharing a protected characteristic within the general student group at a particular disadvantage. It doesn't matter that you did not intend to disadvantage the students with a particular protected characteristic in this way. What does matter is whether your action does or would disadvantage such students compared with students who do not share that characteristic;

- *Discrimination arising from disability* occurs when you treat a disabled student unfavourably because of something connected with their disability and cannot justify such treatment. Discrimination arising from disability is different from direct discrimination. Direct discrimination occurs because of the protected characteristic of disability. For discrimination arising from disability, the reason for the treatment does not matter; the question is whether the disabled student has been treated unfavourably because of something connected with their disability.

There are three types of *harassment* which are unlawful under the Equality Act:

- harassment related to a relevant protected characteristic;
- sexual harassment;
- less favourable treatment of a student because they submit to or reject sexual harassment or harassment related to sex.

Victimisation is defined in the Act as: *treating someone badly because they have done a 'protected act' (or because you believe that a person has done or is going to do a protected act).*

A 'protected act' is:

○ making a claim or complaint of discrimination (under the Equality Act);

○ helping someone else to make a claim by giving evidence or information;

○ making an allegation that you or someone else has breached the Act;

○ doing anything else in connection with the Act.

If you do treat a student less favourably because they have taken such action then this will be unlawful victimisation. There must be a link between what the student did and your treatment of them.

The less favourable treatment does not need to be linked to a protected characteristic.

CHAPTER 3

Activity 1   (Scenario 1 – Teaching Assistant)

Impact on learner

They do not have the English ability to meet the requirements of the course. If the assessment is accurate, they will probably fail the course. The experience could be very demotivating and be a barrier for engaging in education. Learners should never be set up to fail. This learner should be directed on to appropriate alternative courses – such as literacy development – as a step towards meeting their aspiration.

Impact on teacher

This will make teaching very difficult as they will not have the skills to cope with the literacy demands of a level 3 course. While we can differentiate tasks to meet the abilities of learners, this should still be within the framework of the course requirements. Differentiation is not about simplifying tasks to the extent that they do not meet the course requirements. The student could withdraw or fail, having a negative impact on your retention, achievement and progression statistics. If they do pass, this raises questions about the accuracy of initial assessment or the rigour of the level 3 course assessment. Discuss the situation with your manager to ensure that learners are enrolled on to suitable programmes.

Impact on organisation

Although the organisation might meet its recruitment targets, this might have a negative effect on its retention, achievement and progression statistics. The purpose of initial assessment is to make a diagnosis of learners' needs and levels of abilities with the intention of taking appropriate action.

Impact on significant others

A teaching assistant will be working with children. Part of this role is to develop their literacy skills and therefore this needs to be borne in mind when giving consideration to the type and levels of support that the learners could be given.

Suggested solution

Set out a clear path for the learner to progress onto the course. English skills can be developed and this is their priority if they are to meet their career aspirations. Ensure that they are directed to the appropriate department to develop their skills. Comment on the skills that they do have that are appropriate for a teaching assistant course and contact them next year to ask about their progress – to show you are still interested in them joining the course when ready. By doing this, the institution is likely to have an achieving and progressing learner for many years, rather than one who may drop out after a few months.

Activity 2   (Scenario 2 – no initial assessment)

Impact on learner

Learners might enrol on a course that is not suitable for their abilities, causing them to become demotivated, if it is too challenging, or disruptive, if it is not challenging enough and they become bored. If they have needs that are not met, then they may withdraw from the class.

Impact on teacher

You will not be able to plan to meet the needs of your learners. You will only be able to plan a course and then hope that it meets their needs. Once teaching has started, you may need to rapidly change your whole teaching practice. This is an unnecessary waste of time which could have been prevented by doing the job right in the first place. Discuss with your manager the importance of engaging in initial assessment and negotiate a means of implementing this.

Impact on organisation

Learners will be enrolling on inappropriate courses. Special education needs will not be addressed until during the course – which is too late. The institution could face numerous legal challenges for not making reasonable adjustments to meet learner needs.

Possible solution

Initial assessment needs to take place significantly before the start of any course. This is to ensure that the right learners are on the right courses and that teachers have time to adjust their teaching practice to meet the needs of their cohort. As well as this, significant time may be needed for any extra assessments and support organisation for special education needs.

Activity 3   (Scenario 3– new learner introduced halfway through the course)

Impact on learner

The learner is at risk of failing for several reasons. Obviously, they will have missed half of the content so will find it difficult to catch up with the rest of the class. This may also mean that they find it difficult to follow the current activities and could quickly feel demoralised. In addition to this, the class will have developed its own group dynamic – with its own effective ways of working and learning. A newcomer disrupts these established patterns and could therefore slow the development of the group. The learner may feel left out as the other learners already know each other well and have established working relationships.

Impact on teacher

You will only find out any special education needs after the lesson. This means that their first lesson will be potentially inappropriate for the learner and it will be difficult to make any necessary changes to your teaching approaches and resources for future lessons. The learner may not understand key concepts which others are familiar with, and returning to these could waste time. The learner may become disruptive if their lack of understanding and potential isolation from in the group leads to disengagement. As a teacher, you need to identify that this learner is clearly at risk of dropping out of your course and therefore try to take steps to prevent this. This could include extra tutorials, peer learning with more able learners or reviews which focus on any key concepts.

Impact on the organisation

Learners will consider that any organisation rules on attendance are not enforced so class attendance may fall. Allowing learners to join late also devalues the quality of the qualification. Most organisations have attendance policies which this learner is likely to fail to meet. As a teacher, you should firstly negotiate with your manager about when the final date for admission onto any course is. If your organisation has an attendance policy, then this should strengthen your argument.

Possible solution

Ideally, learners should not join during the course. Although it would be difficult to turn away a learner once they have been introduced to the class, you should think about how this could be handled in future. In the meantime, this learner will need extra supervision to ensure that they have some understanding of the task. They could also be paired with a learner who is not just able, but has good social skills to engage in peer learning opportunities. In order to improve practice in the future, you need to change the system, highlighting to colleagues the problems of letting learners enrol throughout the year.

Activity 4   Answers could include keeping records electronically on a shared area so that all relevant stakeholders (other teachers) have access to information about your learners. Remember to adhere to the DPA (1998, amended 2011).

End of chapter reflections   Answers could include:

○   the importance of initial assessment;

○   information about the Equality Act;

○   a requirement to adhere to the DPA;

○   the need to maintain records that are accessible to appropriate others;

○   the importance of planning for learners with different needs.

CHAPTER 4

Activity 1   Possible answers could include the following.

Issues relating to practicality:

○   for the learner, such a long test could cause health and safety issues, such as back problems, eye strain, fatigue. Therefore, this would not be a particularly valid test of language ability as it would be more of an assessment of the learner's endurance ability;

○   it would take hours to complete. Learners may be reluctant/unable to give up this much time;

○   for the teacher, it would take a long time to prepare, though marking could be automatically completed online.

Issues relating to validity:

○   a multiple-choice paper does not replicate real-life experiences using the language – unlike a role play or interview, for example;

○   if the online system is not easy to use, you might be testing IT skills as much as language;

○   it might only test a surface understanding of texts – answers are limited to what is given so there is no opportunity to express deeper understanding;

○   it depends on how many responses are offered: for example, with four choices, by guessing we would achieve a score of around 25 per cent, with two choices 50 per cent, and so on;

○   it depends on the credibility of the other choices – if they are obviously wrong, a learner can guess the correct answer. Conversely, very credible answers can 'trick' the learners – making the test more about spotting misleading writing than about understanding of a subject.

Activity 2   Answers could include, organisational database, regional and national benchmarks, Ofsted, PISA (for international achievements).

Activity 5   Answers could include the use of coloured (often cream or purple) paper or computer screen. Any necessary software could be adjusted to the correct resolutions and accessibility for the learner. Extra time could be provided.

End of chapter reflections   Answers could include:

- knowing more about the principles of assessment;

- an understanding of assessment for and of learning;

- what it means for an assessment to be valid;

- what reliability means;

- different types of assessment.

CHAPTER 5

Activity 1   Communication is the exchange of information using a range of channels including verbal, non-verbal, writing and images.

Activity 2   Shannon and Weaver's model considers noise as an influencing factor, whereas Berlo's model considers communication skills, attitudes, knowledge, social system and cultural factors.

Activity 3   Answers could include:

- background noise;

- visual distractions;

- language differences;

- disabilities.

Activity 7   Complementary transactions are transactions in which the recipient responds in the same ego state as that in which they were addressed. Crossed transactions are transactions in which the recipient responds in a different ego state to that in which they were addressed.

End of chapter reflections   Answers could include:

- the importance of non-verbal communication when engaging with learners and others;

- the different factors that can influence communication with learners and others;

- how to evaluate written resources to ensure their appropriateness for your learners;

- how to evaluate web resources to ensure their appropriateness for your learners;

- the application of transactional analysis in helping to develop evaluation of your communication with learners and others.

CHAPTER 6

Activity 1   An inclusive learning environment is one that is created by a teacher, both physically professionally to ensure that no learners are excluded.

Activity 2   It is important to get to know your learners quickly in order to tailor your teaching to suit their individual needs, ensuring that you are in a position to include them actively in each and every lesson.

Activity 3   Positive reinforcements are the positive effects of behaviours, whereas negative reinforcers are the absence of negative consequences for behaviours.

Activity 4   Answers could include:

○   praise;

○   sweets/chocolates, etc.;

○   certificates;

○   awards.

Activity 5   Once a pattern of acceptable behaviour has been established it can be difficult to break. By establishing clear rules at the start of a course, learners know what is expected of them from the outset.

Activity 6   If learners are actively involved in agreeing rules, they can see their purpose and tend to take ownership of them, leading to a more positive environment in which they are more likely to adhere to the rules.

Activity 7   Intrinsic motivation comes from within the learner, for example, the desire to do something just for the enjoyment of it, whereas extrinsic motivation is provided by external factors, for example, a pay rise, a new job or a qualification.

Activity 8   The Tomlinson Report (1996) contributed to the focus on inclusivity in the FE sector. The report suggested that the approach taken to ensure inclusivity of learners with learning difficulties or disabilities was an approach that could be used to the benefit of all learners.

Activity 9   Your options for rules would vary dependent on your learner; however, you may have recognised that the needs of mature learners may differ. For example, you might insist that a group of 16–18-year-old learners keep their phones in their bags, but allow mature learners to have their phones on the desk, but on a silent setting.

End of chapter reflections   Answers could include:

○   an understanding of ways in which you can provide a safe and inclusive learning environment for your learners;

○   an understanding of how policies and reports influence your approach to inclusive classroom practice;

○   the importance of considering how your learners are motivated and exploration of ways to improve their motivation;

○   the importance of establishing classroom rules with your learners and involving them in the negotiation process;

CHAPTER 7

Activity 1   A teaching and learning plan is a planning document that relates to a single lesson, whereas a scheme of work is a planning document that provides an overview of an entire course

Activity 2   Answers could include:

○   location;

○   numbers of learners;

○   assessment dates;

○   awarding body syllabuses;

○   course length, lesson length or public holidays.

Activity 3   Answers could include:

○   Have you used active verbs?

○   Have you avoided the use of *understand* and *know*?

○   Have you written your objectives using the correct learning domain?

Activity 4   An aim is a statement about what is to be achieved overall, whereas objectives are the steps needed to achieve an aim.

Activity 5   Objectives need to be specific, whereas the word *understand* is very broad and therefore difficult to measure.

Activity 6

○   appreciating a poem – affective domain;

○   learning a language – cognitive domain;

○   changing a tyre – psychomotor domain;

○   writing a story – cognitive domain;

○   decorating a cake – psychomotor domain;

Activity 7   Functional skills are embedded when they are incorporated naturally into a subject-specific lesson, rather than taught as standalone subjects.

Activity 8   Your answers here will differ according to your subject area, but you might have considered some adaptations of the following:

Mathematics: learners could convert between different measurement units, create graphs and charts or perform calculations.

English: language could be developed by getting learners to debate and discuss key course elements, whereas literacy could be developed by composing letters or reports.

ICT: learners could create posters, reports and letters or create a spreadsheet.

Activity 9 The Minimum Core refers to a teacher's skills and knowledge in literacy and language, numeracy and ICT whereas functional skills are learners' skills in mathematics, English and ICT.

Activity 10 Answers could include:

o   age;

o   gender;

o   socio-economic factors;

o   ethnicity;

o   disability or learning difficulty;

o   motivation.

End of chapter reflections Answers could include:

o   the range of planning documentation in FE;

o   the relevance and application of different learning domains when planning courses and lessons;

o   the difference between aims and objectives;

o   how to write SMART objectives;

o   ways to embed functional skills within a range of subject areas;

o   ways to apply knowledge and understanding of the Minimum Core to your lesson planning and delivery.

CHAPTER 8

Activity 4 Often you do not need to provide any paperwork as the mentoring relationship should be confidential. However, you do need to check with your course tutor to see if you need to do more than just set up a mentoring agreement.

Activity 5 This will depend on your experience and what you need from the mentoring relationship. If you are very experienced and not encountering any problems with the course, you might find that you need to meet only infrequently. You could discuss this during your first mentoring lesson and set up a calendar of meetings for the duration of the course, bearing in mind that your needs might change during the course and you might increase or decrease the number of times you meet. It might be that your course specifies how often you should meet.

Activity 6 No, you do not have to observe or be observed by your mentor – unless you have decided this is going to be a useful part of the mentoring process for you.

Activity 7 It is very good practice to have a mentor and they can help enormously. Your course may specify that you have to have to have a mentor. If the mentoring relationship is not working, speak to a line manager or your course tutor. Not all mentoring arrangements work out.

End of chapter reflections   Answers could include:

- requirements for an observation;
- what to expect from a mentor;
- the difference between a formative and a summative observation;
- what the ETF Professional Standards are and how to access the standards;
- how to conduct a peer observation.

CHAPTER 9

End of chapter reflections   Answers could include:

- information about the DET qualification;
- what a SWOT analysis is;
- ways of progressing further;
- where to find information;
- how to complete an Action Plan.

CHAPTER 10

Activity 2

Abbreviation/symbol	Meaning
eg	for example
=	is equal to, the same as
etc.	and so on
≠	is not equal to
cf.	compare
∴	therefore, thus, so
et al.	and others (authors)
∵	because
ibid.	in the same place
+	plus, and, more
N.B. or n.b.	note well
-	minus, less, except
viz	namely, that is to say
>	greater than
<	less than
»	much greater than
«	much less than
≥	at least equal to or greater than
%	per cent

Abbreviation/symbol	Meaning
÷	divide
×	multiply
^	insert
→	from...to, leads to, results in
↑	increases, rises
↓	consequently, decrease, fall
ie	that means, that is
&	and
P or p	page
Sp	spelling
// or para	paragraph
C20	20th century

Source: Staffordshire University (2011)

Activity 3

Class	Definition	Example highlighted in a sentence
Noun	A person, a thing, an idea, quality or state	The *dog* was small.
Pronoun	Use in place of the noun to avoid repetition	The boy was thirsty so *he* had a drink.
Verb	Doing word, what someone or something can do	I *wrote* the assignment.
Adjective	Describes the noun	Bloom's Taxonomy is a classification of learning aims devised in 1956 by a *large* committee of educators chaired by Benjamin Bloom
Adverb	Describes the verb; it can give further information about an adjective or another adverb	They talked *quickly*.
Preposition	The preposition is usually placed before the noun or pronoun to show the relationship with the other words in the sentence	The class starts *at* 10.30am.
Conjunctions	Used to connect sentences, phrases and clauses	They all did their homework *and* managed to watch TV.

Activity 4

1. The principle/~~principal~~ matter is that no one is hurt.

2. I did not mean to imply/~~infer~~ that the learner was lying.

3. They all agreed to complete the homework, ~~accept~~/except for James.

4. The ~~affect~~/effect of the experiment was total destruction.

5. I gave my ~~ascent~~/assent to the field trip.

6. He tried to defuse/~~diffuse~~ the situation by laughing.

7. I will not lose/~~loose~~ my homework.

8. The main building site/~~sight~~ was in a total mess.

9. I need to practise/~~practice~~ my handwriting.

10. She tried to elicit/~~illicit~~ an answer from the quietest learner.

Activity 5

Sentence with relative clause	D or N-D
This is the assignment that I wrote when I was at university.	D
Maslow, whose first name is Abraham, developed the hierarchy of needs theory in 1943.	N-D
This is the behaviourist theory which Skinner innovated.	D
Active learning, which puts the responsibility of learning on learners, was popularised by Bonwell and Eison.	N-D
The assignment which I wrote is very short.	D

End of chapter reflections   Answers could include:

1. The difference between note taking and note making.

2. How to cite others' work in text.

3. The difference between a bibliography and references.

4. A useful list of abbreviations.

5. When and how to use an apostrophe.

Index